IMPROVING POLICE RESPONSE TO PERSONS WITH MENTAL ILLNESS

IMPROVING POLICE RESPONSE TO PERSONS WITH MENTAL ILLNESS

A Progressive Approach

Edited by

THOMAS J. JURKANIN, PH.D.
LARRY T. HOOVER, PH.D.
VLADIMIR A. SERGEVNIN, PH.D.

LAW ENFORCEMENT MANAGEMENT INSTITUTE OF TEXAS SAM HOUSTON STATE UNIVERSITY

ILLINOIS LAW ENFORCEMENT TRAINING & STANDARDS BOARD EXECUTIVE INSTITUTE

CHARLES C THOMAS • PUBLISHER, LTD.
Springfield • Illinois • U.S.A.

Published and Distributed Throughout the World by

CHARLES C THOMAS • PUBLISHER, LTD.
2600 South First Street
Springfield, Illinois 62794-9265

ISBN 978-0-398-07778-5 (pbk.)

Library of Congress Catalog Card Number: 2007025165

With THOMAS BOOKS *careful attention is given to all details of manufacturing and design. It is the Publisher's desire to present books that are satisfactory as to their physical qualities and artistic possibilities and appropriate for their particular use.* THOMAS BOOKS *will be true to those laws of quality that assure a good name and good will.*

Printed in the United States of America
MM-R-3

Library of Congress Cataloging in Publication Data

Improving police response to persons with mental illness : a progressive approach / edited by Thomas J. Jurkanin, Larry T. Hoover, Vladimir Sergevnin.
p. cm.
Includes bibliographical references.
ISBN 978-0-398-07778-5 (pbk.)
1. Police training. 2. Police services for the mentally ill. 3. Mental illness. 4. Mentally ill offenders. 5. Crisis intervention (Mental health services). 6. Police psychology. I. Jurkanin, Thomas J. (Thomas Joseph), 1955– . II. Hoover, Larry T. III. Sergevnin, Vladimir, IV. Title.

HV7923.156 2007
363.2'32--dc22 2007025165

CONTRIBUTORS

LEWIS G. BENDER, PH.D.
Southern Illinois University at Edwardsville

ELIZABETH PERKINS BIEBEL, M.S.
Eastern Kentucky University

GARY W. CORDNER, PH.D.
Eastern Kentucky University

LARRY T. HOOVER, PH.D.
Sam Houston State University

THOMAS J. JURKANIN, PH.D.
Illinois Law Enforcement Training and Standards Board

KAREN C. KALMBACH, PH.D.
Sam Houston State University

PHILIP M. LYONS, JR., J.D., PH.D.
Sam Houston State University

LEONARD W. PECK, JR., PH.D.
Texas A&M University at Texarkana

MELISSA M. REULAND, M.S.
Police Executive Research Forum

MICHELLE Y. RICHTER, PH.D.
Sam Houston State University

KAY E. SCARBOROUGH, PH.D.
Eastern Kentucky University

VLADIMIR A. SERGEVNIN, PH.D.
Western Illinois University

PREFACE

The origins of this book are traceable to two similar tragedies in the states of Illinois and Texas. In both instances the death during a confrontation with the police of a person suffering from mental illness led to both administrative and legislative action. Given legislative concern about the issue, the Illinois Law Enforcement Training and Standards Board convened in the Spring of 2000 a Task Force on Dealing With Persons With Mental Illness. In Illinois, this anthology has its roots in the work of that Task Force. In Texas, legislation required that the Bill Blackwood Law Enforcement Management Institute of Texas (LEMIT) include training addressing interaction with persons with mental illness in the 2006–2007 cycle of its Police Chief's Leadership Series. Development of the content for that Series is the root of this anthology in Texas.

The Illinois Task Force was deliberately constituted to bring together both law enforcement and mental health professionals with three purposes. First, the Task Force was legislatively charged with reviewing current procedures for court-ordered transport of mentally ill persons. Such transport was almost exclusively done by sheriffs' offices in the State of Illinois. Sheriffs throughout the state had expressed concern about the appropriateness of conducting such transport using marked patrol cars and uniformed law enforcement officers. That concern existed as well in the mental health services sector. Second, the Task Force was asked by the Board to review current training for adequacy and appropriateness. Third, the Board asked the Task Force to examine other issues where model policies or procedures might be developed to improve services to persons with mental illness. The Task Force in this respect focused upon interagency agreements between police departments and mental health agencies for both field emergency intervention and temporary housing. The Task Force ultimately developed three related protocols:

- **Statewide Policy Protocol**. The Task Force developed a three-part protocol that is characterized as a "statewide policy protocol." This protocol outlines in broad terms the relationship that should exist between law enforcement agencies and mental health service providers.

- **Model Agency Policy**. The model agency policy is based upon that developed by the Police Executive Research Forum and National Alliance for the Mentally Ill.

- **Model Cooperative Agreement**. The model cooperative agreement was developed by combining features from several existing agreements in the State of Illinois. The primary reference was the City of Champaign agreement.

A special report provides documentation of the proceedings and other deliberations of the Task Force. The primary products are represented among several chapters in this anthology. The effort also included a survey of Illinois law enforcement agencies with respect to the challenges they face in dealing with persons with mental illness. That survey was replicated in the state of Texas, and is described by Leonard Peck in Chapter 3.

The primary charge of the Task Force was the transportation issue. As a result of the Task Force recommendations, the Illinois General Assembly passed Public Act 093-0770 effective January 1, 2005, amending the Illinois Mental Health and Developmental Disabilities Code by adding a provision providing for ambulance transport of a person who is mentally ill in lieu of transportation by the county sheriff. The Act releases the ambulance service for any liability incurred if they act in good faith and without negligence. The Act is designed to provide transportation by medical rather than police conveyance–appropriate to treating mental illness as the disease that it is rather than a "threat to public safety."

In Texas, LEMIT developed an 18-hour unit of instruction for its Chiefs' Leadership Series that was designed to both foster understanding of the attributes of mental illness and suggest "best practices" in developing law enforcement policy and response protocols. The Series is offered on a biennial cycle, and is attended by every chief of police in the state as a requisite for maintaining their certification. Every police chief in Texas had completed the unit of instruction by summer 2007. Additionally, LEMIT published a special issue of its Texas Law Enforcement Management and Administrative Statistics Bulletin series that addressed comparative policies and practices. Like the experience in Illinois, it became evident during the course of LEMIT's efforts that an anthology addressing issues and approaches would be a useful addition to the professional literature in this area.

Certainly a number of excellent resources already exist that address police engagement with persons with mental illness. Among the most important are the following three:

- **Police Response to People with Mental Illnesses**, produced by the Police Executive Research Forum, is a training curriculum and model policy for police agencies that wish to educate their officers about appropriate responses to situations involving people with mental illnesses. The curriculum includes modules–which can be used separately or together–on the Americans with Disabilities Act, types of mental illnesses, treatment options, voluntary and involuntary commitment of people with mental illness, psychiatric evaluations and other situations that police may encounter. It offers techniques and model practices for police officers to deal with a variety of situations, from talking to a person who is experiencing delusions, to transporting a person to a mental health facility for evaluation. PERF, 1997 ISBN: 1-878734-19-9

- **Police Response to People with Mental Illnesses: Video Series**, produced by the Police Executive Research Forum. This is a two-part video on improving the police response to people with mental illness. The first part covers basic information about mental illness, the Americans with Disabilities Act and tips for police dealing with some common types of encounters with people who are mentally ill. The second part focuses on a community policing response to situations involving people with mental illness, including how police can forge partnerships with other service providers to develop long-term resolutions to recurring problems.

- **Criminal Justice/Mental Health Consensus Project Report**, produced by the Council of State Governments, is a comprehensive review of issues across the criminal justice system, including law enforcement. The project is an ongoing effort of the Council of State Governments. Information and the ability to download the report are available at http://www.consensusproject.org/.

Nevertheless, it was evident that a book that systematically explored issues and problems would be an important addition to the literature base. We have not attempted to reproduce the policy and training guidelines that are available from the resource documents above. Rather, this anthology provides a more "issue-oriented" discussion of current developments, trends, and emerging protocols to improve services provided by law enforcement to persons with mental illness.

A long-standing cooperative relationship exists between the Illinois Law Enforcement Executive Institute, an entity of the Illinois Law Enforcement Training and Standards Board, and the Law Enforcement Management Institute of Texas, a program of Sam Houston State University. Concurrently, both entities recognized the need for this anthology in the police literature base. Given the concurrent developmental effort on the issues, and given the long-standing cooperative relationship, co-sponsorship of this anthology was logical.

CONTENTS

IMPROVING POLICE RESPONSE TO PERSONS WITH MENTAL ILLNESS

Part I

The Origins of the Problem

Chapter 1

ATYPICAL SITUATIONS–ATYPICAL RESPONSES

LARRY T. HOOVER

Are police "uncaring" toward persons suffering from mental illness? A statewide summit on the issue of police interaction with persons with mental illness was the focus of a conference convened in Bloomington, Illinois, in November 2002, sponsored by the Illinois Law Enforcement Training and Standards Board. As is typical with that type of meeting, the 100 participants were broken into smaller groups and assigned specific issues to discuss, then report back in a plenary session. Although most groups consisted of a mix of mental health professionals and police managers, given its assignment my particular group was all mental health professionals. During the course of the group discussion, references were made on several occasions to the uncaring attitude of the police toward mentally ill persons, and what might be done about it.

My personal experience is that the police are not at all callous toward the plight of persons with mental illness. Indeed, they are extremely sympathetic. Yes, there are locker room comments that involve the use of colloquial terms that are inappropriate, but I have never personally witnessed police officers interacting with someone in such distress in a calloused way. I finally raised the issue–noting that my experience did not match the perception of the mental health professionals that the police were indeed callous about victims of mental illness. The response is a quintessential illustration of variation in human perception. The explanation provided was that the only concern of police officers with whom the mental health professionals dealt was to "get rid of" the patient. I inquired specifically as to whether anyone had ever witnessed a police officer being abusive toward a person with mental illness, and the answer was "no." Instead, the perception that the police are callous was derived entirely from the observation that officers just wanted to get "back into service," and really weren't concerned what kind of treatment the person received–just so they didn't have to "bother with them."

The public, including mental health professionals, little appreciate the need for police officers to stay available for genuine 911 emergencies. Rather than a calloused attitude, officer behavior is explained by the fact that they are under enormous pressure to remain available on patrol. The perception that patrol officers are callous toward persons with mental illness is incorrect. Indeed, Cooper et al.'s survey data led them to conclude that:

> Police are often branded as insensitive to the needs of mentally ill persons, but these results suggest the opposite. Additionally, respondents indicated a desire for more training in working with such persons, suggesting that not only do they feel responsible for working with the mentally ill, but they also wish to do so in a quality fashion. (2004)

However, quality response conflicts with the need to stay "in-service." When a call for service exceeds 30 minutes, there is pressure to return to service. When a call for service exceeds an hour, there is strong pressure. When a call for service exceeds two hours, the lieutenant wants to know "what's wrong?" Taking custody of persons with severe mental illness is inherently a time-consuming process. Frequently, the on-scene interaction is time-consuming. The paperwork involved in an involuntary commitment is extensive. Further, in many jurisdictions there is difficulty in finding an appropriate person or facility to which the patient can be "handed off." Thus, patrol officers are often left monitoring the patient until a bed can be found–sometimes literally for hours. Reinforcing this perspective, LaFond (1996) suggested police officers use jails more frequently because booking takes less time than commitment. Indeed, an average hospitalization commitment was found to take two and one-half hours versus less than one hour for an arrest (Green, 1997). Phelan and Link (1998) report that as an outgrowth of concern that accompanied deinstitutionalization, 36 of 50 states imposed more stringent criteria for civil commitment. As a matter of public policy the civil commitment process is not intended to be "simple." An unintended consequence is that if an offense has occurred, no matter how trivial, it is often more expedient to "just book'em."

Both the Mental Health and Police Professions Face Parallel Social Dynamics

1. They both deal with intractable problems without ultimate solutions.
2. Their workflow is like a river, not a lake. No matter how hard you bail, the water just keeps on coming.
3. Larger social, economic, and political environments define the problems with which each must deal. The professions can influence only marginally the larger impacting environment.
4. Both deal with a rich clientele mix. There are those clients who love us and are eternally grateful for our help, and those who regard us as "the enemy."
5. Each profession has both prevention and treatment as part of its mandate.
6. There is ostensible strong public support for the goals of each–but real limitations at budget time.
7. "I would not want to do your job" is a typical public reaction to doing the daily work required of both.
8. But among those who do the job–"I would not have chosen another profession" is a more typical reaction.

Serving as first responders during mental health crises is a longstanding law enforcement responsibility. Indeed, there are wide ranges of police responsibilities that do not relate to their crime control function. Many police agencies are referred to as "departments of public safety"–underscoring the breadth of their role. Functions such as traffic flow regulation, delivering death notices, conflict management, addressing community quality of life issues, responding to safety threats and managing responses to natural disasters are all illustrations of the breadth of law enforcement's role. Among the "legitimate" safety functions of the police is dealing with persons with mental illness. The police function as first responders to numerous medical emergencies. Police training includes medical first responder curriculum. However, intervention in situations where a person with mental illness is delusional, hallucinating, feeling very threatened, fearful, or disoriented, challenges law enforcement skills. Despite the fact that such response is recognized as part of the role of law enforcement, interaction with persons with serious mental illness is an atypical situation requiring atypical responses.

Why Mentally Ill Persons Are Atypical Situations

TOO MUCH TIME. The need to clear a call quickly, whether the need is very real or simply perceived, has several ramifications for interaction between police officers and persons with mental illness. First, it, too, often results in officers minimizing the seriousness of the situation. If behaviors are judged life-threatening, then a long and tedious process of custody and commitment is triggered. Since violence is in reality a relatively rare event among persons with mental illness (Swanson, Swartz and Elbogen, 2004), it is easy for a patrol officer to rationalize that "this isn't likely going to be all that serious," and simply counsel the person to settle down, and leave. Second, if the situation is such that custody is necessary, police officers have a tendency to rush to physical restraint. That is, rather than take the time to quietly and patiently counsel to obtain voluntary compliance, officers, too, often seize upon the first opportunity "throw the cuffs on." This is, after all, what they would do in other circumstances involving problematic persons, and it is easy to understand why they might use the same approach with a person suffering from mental illness. It is quicker. Third, officers are frequently reluctant to call for professional outside emergency intervention assistance. In particular, if an agency does not have a standing mutual aid agreement with a mental health service provider, officers will hesitate to invoke this process. Whether a mutual aid agreement exists or not, it means standing by at the scene for at least 30 minutes until a professional emergency counselor arrives. What is likely to go through an officer's mind is that "My whole shift is gonna be shot, and I'll just see this guy back out on the street again a week from now anyway." Fourth, when custody is invoked and commitment is sought, mental health professionals are likely to encounter police officers who are frustrated and inpatient. Again, "This isn't real police work–I'm not preventing any crime–and I'm tied up for the whole shift." The officer's view of the whole situation is, after all, that this should not be the role of law enforcement, but mental health professionals. Adding to their frustration, is a lack of bed space. Officers often make the rounds of mental health service agencies–from the halfway house to the hospital to the detox center–before resorting to arrest (Teplin, 2000). An attitude soon develops characterized by the phrase "What am I doing here?" From one perspective, is the officer wrong?

There is, of course, a very legitimate response to the "What am I doing here?" pondering of a police officer. Scholars and progressive police managers have long recognized that the real role of the police is not crime control, but the broader mandate of order maintenance. A person who is seriously mentally ill is certainly a disorderly situation. Failure to intervene on the part of law enforcement can sometimes result in tragedy–a frequent form of which is suicide. Further, neither mental health professionals, nor emergency medical personal are prepared to deal with instances when a person with mental illness becomes violent. Physical control by law enforcement comes first in such situations, medical intervention next. All that having been said, the average cop on the street seldom sees it this way. Their self-perception is that of a crime fighter, and persons with mental illness are not criminals–an attitude, by the way, that we would endorse. So although the police are sympathetic and compassionate, an individual officer's goal is typically to "get outta here" as fast as possible.

Training for law enforcement is address in Chapter 7. Certainly, training can contribute substantially to changing patrol officer attitudes. Training should emphasize, of course, appropriate interactive techniques to employ, but training can and should also include broader philosophical issues–the "What are we doing here?" issue.

USE OF FORCE. Tragic incidents too often arise when the police confront a person with mental illness who is armed. When a mentally ill person has a gun in her/his hands, and is threatening to shoot or even has already shot others, the police have little choice. How else did we expect the U.S. Capital police to respond when Russell Weston invaded the building in July 1998, killing two police officers? But it is also true that in numerous instances the police taking the life of a person with mental illness, even someone who is "armed," is unnecessary. No responsible police official would defend the actions of an officer who shoots a seriously deranged woman from a distance of 15 feet simply because she is standing with a small knife in her hand. Such an instance actually occurred recently–it is not hypothetical. The substantial majority of tragic incidents fall somewhere between these two extremes.

Muir in his landmark book, *Police: Street Corner Politicians* (1977) offers an analysis of the law enforcement role from a social psychology perspective. Muir notes that there is one guiding principle to police interaction with citizens–maintenance of control by the police officer. Control requires the officer to be able to predict accurately the actions of the citizen. The issue for a police officer is not whether a given citizen is courteous and respectful or belligerent and hostile. The issue is the predictability of the behavior. When officers approach gang members who they know will be belligerent and hostile, they respond accordingly with due caution. Depending upon the circumstance, police weapons are either at the ready or actually drawn. In contrast, a traffic stop for a minor violation involving a woman driving a minivan with five kids in soccer uniforms in the backseats is very likely to involve a fundamentally cooperative citizen and the officer will respond accordingly. Problematic situations occur for the police when they cannot reliably predict the behavior to be encountered. Interaction with persons with mental illness very frequently is unpredictable and hence stressful for the police. Thus, when an officer on patrol hears on the radio "1 Adam 12 respond to First and Main, subject apparently mentally ill," the officer's reaction is not, "Oh joy, how exciting, how interesting, this call has just made my day." Instead, the reaction is far more likely to be "Dispatch, couldn't you have 2 Adam 13 take that call, I'm busy observing a traffic light."

The Safety Issue

The rate of violence among seriously mentally ill persons who are hallucinating or delusional is higher than the general population (Junginger and McGuire, 2004). Swanson et al. note that: "While the great majority of persons with schizophrenia do not commit violent acts, clinicians recognize that some individuals with this disorder may pose a significant risk in the community. . ." (2004). Thus, concern for safety by police officers is real and justified in many situations. When a mentally ill person is in a highly irrational state of mind, the chances of the police officer having to use force presumably increase and with it the possibility of injury to both the officer and the civilian increases as well (Adams, 1999). The stress of greater risk in some situations and unpredictability in even more frequently leads to overreaction by officers.

Police officers do not throw handcuffs on every citizen with whom they interact. Though that might strike the reader as a simplistic observation, it has important implications. The police are trained to use physical restraint only when there is clear and present danger–only when there is clear justification for doing so. If an officer pulls our soccer mom from the car and throws handcuffs on her during a minor traffic stop just to be sure she is not a threat, one could be assured that public outcry would be strong and persistent. Similarly, we do not, and the police do not want to put handcuffs on a mentally ill citizen who is not violent, not dangerous, and simply very sick. Ninety-nine percent of the police officers in the United States of America would not want to employ such physical restraint in these circumstances even if it were clearly allowed by policy, but officers, particularly youthful officers, face the predictability problem. Inexperienced officers tend to use force more often (Terrill and Mastrofski, 2002). In situations involving persons who are mentally ill, the reason may well be inexperience with behavior prediction. Will the person with mental illness remain calm and composed? If someone is seriously ill and out of touch with reality, can I trust them to stay calm and collected?

Further, it must be understood that the police are concerned about more than their own personal safety. They do not want to hurt anyone. The cynics would say, "Yeah, cause it's four hours worth of paperwork." That is indeed true; it is four hours of hated paperwork, but police officers are normal human beings, and normal human beings do not want to hurt other human beings. Thus, they have to take into account whether they can easily control an unrestrained citizen who suddenly becomes violent without hurting the citizen in order to subdue them.

An even more problematic situation is a mentally ill person who is overtly suicidal. A person holding a knife, or worse yet holding a gun–whether pointed at themselves or at the ground–is a serious threat to a police officer. Muir notes that persons that are most dreaded by the police are those who "have nothing to lose." Police officers know quite well that a person who no longer places any value on their own life is not likely to place much value on someone else's life. A police officer with any longevity has likely responded to a murder/suicide incident.

Given the totality of the circumstances surrounding police interaction with persons with mental illness, it should not surprise us that the police frequently throw on the cuffs far earlier than is necessary.

Pinning on the badge means acceptance of some level of risk. No police officer truly thinks they ever might be counted in the FBI's "officers killed in the line of duty" list. Nevertheless, there is recognition among police officers that the role is inherently dangerous. Officers are not going to approach situations with wanton disregard for their own well-being. They will take precautions. Indeed, precautionary techniques are drilled into police recruits during academy training. We expect and want law enforcement officers to use reasonable caution, but a balance must be attained. While a few seriously mentally ill persons may pose a risk, research indicates that statistically impairment by mental illness does not correlate with higher rates of necessary use of force (Kaminski et al., 2004). That is, "attack" rates on police officers are not higher from persons who are suffering from mental illness. In a survey of 164 Pennsylvania police agencies, 93 percent reported that police officers were never or seldom injured, and on occasions when injury occurred 89 percent of the time medical attention was not required (Ruiz and Miller, 2004). Therefore, statistically, these are not disproportionately dangerous situations for police officers. Perhaps the rates of violent interaction are not higher because officers use more precaution, so one must be careful drawing policy conclusions. What can be said, however, is that "balance" with regard to force and physical restraint (handcuffs) in police and mentally ill person interactions is appropriate.

Types of Interaction

Law enforcement agencies are called to intervene in numerous types of mental health situations. Ruiz and Miller (2004) report that 7.2 percent of all calls for service involve persons with mental illness. So police interaction with persons with mental illness is common. Among the circumstances are:

- Mentally ill person is the victim of a crime or accident.
- Mentally ill person is the perpetrator of a crime.
- Family, friends or other concerned persons call the police for assistance during a psychiatric crisis.

- A citizen calls the police because they feel threatened by unusual behavior or the mere presence of a person with mental illness.
- Mental health agencies or hospitals call for security when a client is disruptive.
- Mental health agencies or hospitals call for assistance with transport.
- Mentally ill person calls the police for assistance because imaginative threats exist.
- Mentally ill person feels suicidal and calls the police as a cry for help.
- Street encounter with a mentally ill person behaving inappropriately.
- Court order or petition to detain, commit, or transport a person with mental illness.
- Physician petition or certification to detain or transport a person with mental illness.

Police concern in all of these situations is protection of both the general citizenry and, very importantly, the person afflicted with mental illness.

Tragic incidents involving police use of deadly force are all too common. Two recent incidents in Illinois focused public attention in that state on the problem of police interaction with persons with mental illness. Given these incidents, and given legislative concern about the issue, in the spring of 2000 the Illinois Law Enforcement Training and Standards Board convened a Task Force on Dealing with Persons with Mental Illness. To assist the Task Force this author conducted a survey of Illinois law enforcement agencies with regard to the interaction dynamics with persons with mental illness. The survey was repeated in the state of Texas by Leonard Peck. The results from both states are reported in detail in Chapter 3. Results of the analysis reveal that, overall, the respondents most often encounter a situation where family, friends, or other concerned persons call the police for assistance during a psychiatric crisis. The second most frequent type of encounter is when a citizen calls the police because they feel threatened by unusual behavior or the mere presence of a person with mental illness. Almost as frequently, police experience "street encounters" with a mentally ill person behaving inappropriately. It should be noted that responding to court orders or physician certification to detain or transport a person with mental illness occurs much less frequently.

The survey of Illinois and Texas law enforcement agencies also included a query with regard to the difficulty for patrol officers in dealing with the range of situations delineated above. The situation that most respondents rated as very difficult and very stressful for officers is a person with mental illness who feels suicidal and calls the police as a cry for help. This is hardly surprising, since these are indeed always life or death situations. However, it should also be noted that responding agencies also indicated several other types of encounters as being difficult and stressful for officers. These included situations involving a street encounter with a mentally ill person behaving inappropriately, and when family, friends or other concerned persons call the police for assistance during a psychiatric crisis. This is important to note because, unlike most law enforcement situations, in this case the most frequently encountered situations are also the most stressful situations. As a rule, high-stress situations are also low frequency situations.

Should Dirty Harry Also Be a Counselor?

First and foremost, we expect the police to be as effective as possible in preventing crime, and as efficient as possible in solving it. Is it reasonable to expect them to be mental health diagnosticians and counselors as well? Probably not. What we do want from police officers in dealing with persons with mental illness is, first of all, compassion. We want them to recognize that the person is suffering from an illness. We want them to realize that problematic behaviors are not willful, that the person could not simply "straighten out" if they truly wanted to. We want them to recognize that in cases of serious mental illness professional assistance should be sought. We do not want them to walk away from situations that merit intervention simply because intervening requires too much time or trouble.

A comparison with another role of law enforcement might be useful here. Part of the police traffic responsibility is to assist stranded motorists. Citizens will be very unhappy if a marked patrol unit simply cruises by when they are sitting on the edge of a road with their hood up. Since the advent of the cell phone obtaining roadside assistance is not quite the issue it once was, but it is still a stressful situation.

During my years as a police officer I gained important insight about how to make roadside assistance contacts a very successful police citizen interaction, and conversely how to make it very unsuccessful. If I pulled the patrol car to the side of the road behind the stranded motorist, engaged the motorist in conversation, learned that the engine had stalled and wouldn't start, and then simply offered to call a wrecker, citizens were inevitably quite irritated. There was an expectation that a police officer possessed skill in auto repair. Citizens often perceive that police officers possess skills that they do not. What I learned to do was to have the motorist pop the hood, if it was not already up, instruct them to stay in the driver's seat, bend over the engine and start "tinkering around." Once or twice I would straighten up and instruct them to try turning the engine over again. In the meantime I would make a considerable amount of noise banging on black boxes that I had no idea did what. Since the driver's view would be obstructed by the open hood, it really would not matter what I did, just so I made some noise. After a couple of minutes of this I would return to the motorist and pronounce in an authoritative voice, "It looks pretty serious to me, I guess we are going to have to call a wrecker." Inevitably, the stranded motorist would express gratitude for my assistance and be perfectly happy with resorting to calling the tow truck.

The point of my light-hearted war story, and it is absolutely true, is that the public often has expectations that the police cannot meet. That having been said, we should expect police officers to handle persons with mental illness with compassion and indeed even with some skill, but our expectations have to reasonable. Even mental health professionals experience difficulty in handling someone who is seriously ill. There is a real and compelling need for cooperative agreements with mental health service providers as described in Chapter 8. The police role is emergency intervention to gain control of a situation. It should not exceed that. Once a situation is no longer overtly dangerous, it is time to call a wrecker, not attempt to repair the engine. A mentally ill person should be in the hands of a mental health professional as soon as possible.

Role of Cooperative Agreements

A cooperative agreement should be in place between law enforcement agencies and mental health service providers. See Chapters 8 and 10 for a complete discussion of such agreements. The cooperative agreement should include provisions for summoning a mental health professional to a field setting whenever a mentally ill person is exhibiting problematic behavior. It is assumed that such situations frequently incorporate involuntary commitment, and attendant transportation. The cooperative agreement should also delineate procedures for temporary detention of a mentally ill person in a mental health facility. Law enforcement managers frequently complain that patrol officers are required to wait several hours while commitment processes are completed at a mental health facility. The cooperative agreement should contain provisions to eliminate untoward delay in these circumstances. As noted elsewhere in this chapter, maintaining a field presence is no small matter for a police agency. When units are out of service they are unable to respond to not only routine requests for police assistance, but emergency calls as well. Returning units to service in a timely manner is an endemic problem for law enforcement managers. A cooperative agreement can assist in eliminating the problem in mental health commitment cases.

It should be emphasized that there is more involved to cooperation than simply drafting a cooperative agreement. It is imperative that working relationships be developed between police organizations and mental health agencies. Representatives of both mental health and law enforcement agencies from entities with existing agreements have voiced enthusiasm about the value of the agreements, and the importance of the close working relationship the agreements foster. Five important goals of cooperative agreements are:

1. Prevent tragedy or physical harm to persons with mental illness.
2. Prevent tragedy or physical harm to law enforcement personnel as well as inappropriate release of persons who subsequently harm themselves or others.
3. Encourage referral for long-term intervention and treatment.
4. Maintain the dignity of the person suffering from mental illness, particularly avoiding when possible the stigma of arrest.
5. Serve as a governmental role model for the rest of society, treating mental illness as an illness.

Among the provisions of a model cooperative agreement is that a mental health professional should be summoned to a field setting when problematic behaviors are exhibited. However, whether a cooperative agreement exists or not, it should be standard police policy to summon professional assistance in these situations. Police officers are ill-equipped to deal with the sensitive counseling skills that are required when dealing with a seriously mentally ill person. Indeed, as noted in the training literature (see Chapter 7), standard police procedures in these situations are often counterproductive. Officers are trained to gradually escalate authoritative commands when a citizen is noncompliant. In cases with seriously mentally ill persons, such procedures often aggravate the situation rather than achieve compliance. The way in which law enforcement personnel–or mental health professionals–communicate with a person in crisis can either escalate or de-escalate the situation (Jurkanin et al., 2003). No one would argue that special training is required to deal with a person who is delusional, suffering from hallucinations, or so deeply depressed as to be suicidal.

It is frequently not cost-effective to train every patrol officer to the depth necessary to deal with these situations. Further, even if such training could be offered, the number of instances in which the skills are employed are rare enough that the skills taught might be lost before they could be used. Hence, most agencies that have addressed the issue have developed mental health crisis intervention teams. The teams receive in-depth training. See Chapters 7 and 9 for a complete discussion of this issue.

Law Enforcement Agency Policy

The survey instrument distributed to Illinois law enforcement agencies indicated extensive use of community mental health centers. Over half (53%) indicated that in noncustodial situations that nevertheless require long-term intervention, law enforcement agencies normally contact mental health centers. Some 22 percent would contact a hospital in this situation, although it should be noted that many hospitals have mental health wards that operate as a community mental health center. However, a surprisingly low percentage of Illinois agencies had a formal agreement or protocol with a community mental health center or hospital–only 26 percent. On the parallel survey of Texas agencies similar results were obtained–only 7 of 40 agencies had such agreements, 18 percent (see Chapter 3). In Illinois, only 17 percent had a written policy statement concerning interaction with mentally ill persons. The utility of both a model cooperative agreement and a model agency policy is self-evident.

There are two equally important levels of model policy. First, police agencies should review the model policy jointly produced by the Police Executive Research Forum (PERF) and the National Alliance for the Mentally Ill (NAMI), modify it as deemed appropriate for their agency, and formally adopt it as part of the agency's policy documents. The model policy recommended by PERF/NAMI includes the following major elements:

- Purpose
- Policy
- Definitions
- Procedures
- Recognizing Abnormal Behavior
  - Determining Danger
  - Dealing with the Mentally Ill
  - Taking Custody or Making Referral
- Policy Recommendations
  - Symptoms of Mental Illness
  - Other Causes of Abnormal Behavior
  - Police Response to the Mentally Ill
  - Approaching and Handling the Mentally Ill
  - Taking Custody or Making Referral

The policy is intended to be a comprehensive statement of both agency philosophy and specific procedures addressing interaction between law enforcement officers and persons with mental illness.

Victimization of Persons with Mental Illness

There is considerable concern both in the law enforcement and mental health communities with regard to criminal victimization of persons with mental illness (Hiday et al., 2002). Persons with mental illness are vulnerable for several reasons. They may be singled out because predators perceive that they are less able to defend themselves or cry for help. They may not recognize dangerous situations as well as others, and "walk into" circumstances that others would avoid. Persons who are mentally ill who are homeless present obvious targets for predators. Some persons who are mentally ill are more easily persuaded than other citizens, and may be the victim of fraud or other schemes. Most agencies indicated that persons with mental illness were indeed more likely to be victimized. The ratings for several offenses, however, were not inordinately high–that is, responding agencies did not feel that persons with mental illness were far more likely to be victimized, only somewhat more likely. However, agencies consistently reported far higher victimization rates for sexual assault. Further, a number of the comments in the open-ended questions underscored this point.

Police agencies over the last decade have consistently moved toward a technique called problem-oriented policing. The core idea is to attempt an interdiction that prevents a problem from recurring, rather than simply responding to a given incident at hand. This frequently involves crime prevention techniques, victim education, nuisance abatement efforts, or even structural redesign of streets or buildings. The issue of increased likelihood of victimization among persons with mental illness lends itself to problem-oriented intervention techniques.

Transportation of Persons with Mental Illness

Concern has been raised on numerous occasions regarding the appropriateness of using law enforcement officers to transport persons with mental illness who refuse voluntary commitment, and for whom a court order has been issued requiring incapacitation (Steadman et al., May 2001) . Although hypothetically municipal police agencies might engage in such transport, as a practical matter ninety-nine percent are performed by county sheriff's departments. The transport typically involves the dispatch of two deputies to the home of the person with mental illness, removal from the home, by force if necessary, placement of the person in the back of a patrol car, and transport to a designated mental health facility, sometimes minutes away and sometimes an hour or two away. Sheriff's departments traditionally perform this function for two reasons.

First, there is simply no one else to do it. Although from one perspective such transport occurs routinely, it does not occur frequently enough to create an independent governmental agency to perform the function. In theory, such an agency might be created on a statewide basis, with enough transport required to occupy several units full-time. However, it is clear that an enormous amount of time would be spent in transit for any such agency. Further, the emergency nature of many of these detentions would make it necessary to, unless the agency were very heavily staffed, periodically employ law enforcement for such transport anyway.

Second, although it is rare, on occasion a person with mental illness becomes violent when subjected to forced removal from their home. When such a situation occurs, the training and equipment possessed by law enforcement officers is an important attribute for the government agents involved in forcible removal. Very few would suggest that a typical ambulance crew would be prepared to routinely handle such situations.

On the other hand no one is happy about law enforcement officers performing this task. Sheriff's departments do not want to perform the task. Partially, it is simply a resource question. The function ties up two deputies for several hours each time it is performed. Additionally, however, law enforcement shares with the mental health profession disdain for the concept of police officers intervening in a health matter. No one would ever suggest that law enforcement agencies be sent to the home of an individual suffering from liver disorder, kidney disorder, or any other health problem of a physical nature. We now recognize mental illness as a brain disorder. It is inherently offensive to subject a person enduring the pain of mental illness to procedures designed for the transport of criminal offenders. Every effort should be made to find alternate transport. In order of preference, transportation of a person with mental illness to a mental health facility should be by

1. Personal vehicle driven by family or friends
2. Ambulance
3. Ambulance accompanied by a peace officer
4. Unmarked police vehicle
5. Marked police vehicle

At the very least, marked police vehicles should not be routinely employed for transportation. Ideally, they are a last resort. No one is happy about placing a mentally ill person in the caged backseat of a police car. While it is recognized that there may be circumstances where transportation by a patrol vehicle is necessary, it should be every agency's policy to use such a mode of transportation only when absolutely necessary.

As noted in the Preface, the Illinois General Assembly passed Public Act 093-0770 effective January 1, 2005, amending the Illinois Mental Health and Developmental Disabilities Code by adding a provision providing for ambulance transport of a person who is mentally ill in lieu of transportation by the county sheriff. The Act is designed to provide transportation by medical rather than police conveyance–appropriate to treating mental illness as the disease that it is rather than a "threat to public safety."

Detention

Detention of mentally ill persons in jails and prisons is a national disgrace. A recent literature review suggests that six percent to fifteen percent of persons in jails have severe mental illness (Cooper et al., 2004). It is not the fault of law enforcement agencies. This is a national political issue, and will require legislative action. Police professionals decry the situation as much as mental health professionals. Law enforcement agencies do not detain individuals simply because they are mentally ill, or even for unusual behavioral patterns. Even those taken into custody under "protection of self or others" emergency detention provisions are taken to a mental health facility unless it is impossible to do so. The issue is arrest for petty offenses, when the root cause of the behavior is mental illness. Our jails have become *de facto* temporary holding facilities for thousands of mentally ill persons, frequently homeless, who have committed minor violations of the law. No one is more unhappy with the situation than county sheriffs–they assert to a person that mentally ill persons should not be in our county jails. The offenses for which they are incarcerated are frequently solely a product of symptoms of their illness. When the offenses are not felonious, other interventions are clearly more appropriate.

Summary

The contributors to *Police Engagement with Persons with Mental Illness* have made a conscious effort to avoid platitudes, and offer instead concrete recommendations. There will always be tragic incidents when the police must be summoned to deal with an inherently medical situation. However, the number of such incidents can be dramatically reduced by the administrative actions suggested in this anthology. Additionally, the quality of life for persons with mental illness, particularly those inappropriately caught up in the criminal justice system, can be dramatically improved through the public policy and legislative changes discussed. It is tragic that the astounding progress made in pharmaceutical treatment of mental illness has been matched step-by-step by regression in the social treatment of the disease through relegation of suffering persons to the criminal justice system.

REFERENCES

Adams, K. (1999). What we know about police use of force. In National Institute of Justice (Ed.), *Use of force by police: Overview of national and local data* (pp. 1–14). Washington, DC: National Institute of Justice.

Cooper, V. G., McLearen, A. M., & Zapf, P. A. (2004, September). Dispositional decisions with the mentally ill: Police perceptions and characteristics. *Police Quarterly,* 7(3), 295–310.

Green, T. M. (1997). Police as frontline mental health workers: The decision to arrest or refer to mental health agencies. *International Journal of Law and Psychiatry, 20,* 469–486.

Hiday, V. A., Swartz, M. S., Swanson, J. W., Borum, R., & Wagner, H. R. (1999, January 7). Criminal victimization of persons with severe mental illness. *Psychiatric Services, 50,* 62–68.

Hiday, V. A., Swartz, M. S., Swanson, J. W., Borum, R., & Wagner, H. R. (2002, August). Impact of outpatient commitment on victimization of people with severe mental illness. *American Journal of Psychiatry, 159,* 1403–1411.

Junginger, J., & McGuire, L. (2004). Psychotic motivation and the paradox of current research on serious mental illness and rates of violence. *Schizophrenia Bulletin, 30*(1), 21–30.

Jurkanin, T. J., Sergevnin, V. A., & Bender, L. G. (2003). *White paper. Modernizing mental health and law enforcement traditional collaboration: Health and enforcing law providers (HELP) units.* Springfield, IL: Illinois Law Enforcement Training and Standards Board.

Kaminski, R. J., DiGiovanni, C., & Downs, R. (2004, September). The use of force between the police and persons with impaired judgment. *Police Quarterly,* 7(3), 311–338.

LaFond, J. Q. (1996). The impact of law on the delivery of involuntary mental health services. In B. D. Sales & D. W. Shuman (Eds.), *Law, mental health, and mental disorder* (pp. 219–239). Pacific Grove, CA: Brooks/Cole.

Muir, W. K. (1977). *Police: Street corner politicians.* University of Chicago Press.

Phelan, J., & Link, B. (1998). The growing belief that persons with mental illness are violent: The role of the dangerousness criterion for civil commitment. *Social Psychiatry, 33,* S7–S12.

Ruiz, J., & Miller, C. (2004, September). An exploratory study of Pennsylvania police officers' perceptions of dangerousness and their ability to manage persons with mental illness. *Police Quarterly, 7*(3), 359–371.

Steadman, H., Deane, M., Borum, R., & Morrissey, J. (2000, May). Comparing outcomes of major models of police responses to mental health emergencies. *Psychiatric Services, 51*(5), 99–101.

Swanson, J. W., Swartz, M. S., & Elbogen, E. B. (2004). Effectiveness of atypical antipsychotic medications in reducing violent behavior among persons with schizophrenia in community-based treatment. *Schizophrenia Bulletin, 30*(1), 3–20.

Teplin, L. A. (2000, July). Keeping the peace: Police discretion and mentally ill persons. *National Institute of Justice Journal,* 9–15.

Terrill, W., & Mastrofski, S. D. (2002, June). Situational and officer-based determinates of police coercion. *Justice Quarterly, 19*(2), 215–248.

Chapter 2

COMMUNITY TREATMENT AND THE POLICE

MICHELLE Y. RICHTER

Police encounters with persons who are mentally ill happen every day. When mishandled, everyone loses; family members mourn the loss of loved ones, police officers are involved with deadly encounters, and police departments must address public outrage. What of the community that calls the police to handle these cases but abhors the outcome? It settles into unease that this could happen to one of their own and simultaneously solidifies beliefs that persons who are mentally ill are dangerous and must be dealt with appropriately.

> On October 29th, 2001 four police officers responded to the desperate call made by a sister who could no longer control her 38-year-old brother. The sister had originally called mental health authorities for help but had been transferred to 911 by the operator. Her brother had been diagnosed with bipolar disorder thirteen years earlier and recently had manifested paranoia and delusions in response to the September 11th terrorist attacks. She begged the police to help him, not hurt him. Officers found the man in the back yard waving a screwdriver. He did not obey their orders to drop the weapon. After being shot with a beanbag gun, the man climbed on top of a doghouse still waving the screwdriver. Officers opened fire, one emptying his entire clip and reloading. In its entirety the incident lasted five minutes. Fourteen shots, six in the back were fired and the brother was dead. The police department claimed the shooting was justified. (Khanna, 2004)

Unfortunately, this story is not an isolated incident. Tragedy too often results from police interaction with persons with mental illness. In order to fully comprehend this complex interaction of beliefs and outcomes, it is important to understand the nature and prevalence of mental illness, identify who provides for the treatment of persons who are mentally ill, and specify desired outcomes for typical situations in which police are called to deal with persons with mental illness.

The values, training, and experiences of police officers have a direct impact on how calls are handled and the disposition options they invoke. Are persons who are mentally ill viewed by police as dangerous, nuisances, or citizens in need? The answer to this question alone can influence departmental guidelines, provide a climate for particular police responses, or stimulate the development of specialized units for mental health crises (Bittner, 1967; Gillig et al., 1990; Steadman et al., February, 2001). Police interactions with this portion of the community require more than the typical response to criminal offenders. Investigation into the context of mental illness provides insight into why tragedies such as the one above occur and how they may be prevented in the future.

Prevalence of Mental Illness in the Community

The reality is that mental illness is far more prevalent than most people wish to recognize. The term "mental illness" refers to a host of maladies that may affect the functioning of the human brain. These afflictions may be biological in origin, the result of injury or insult to the brain, or the cognitive response to overwhelming experiences such as death of a loved one. Research indicates that psychological disorders may be so common that as many as one in three may be affected to varying degrees (Robins, Locke and Regier, 1991). It is best to think of mental illness in terms of a continuum with some individuals being highly functional in daily life at one end with those highly debilitated and unable to function on the other. To paint a bleaker picture, research indicates that over 60 percent of individuals who report one disorder will experience two or more additional disorders in their life time (Kessler et al. 1994). Those with severe mental illness face chronic, reoccurring episodes with "profound disrupt[ion] of a person's thinking, feeling, moods, ability to relate to others and capacity for coping with the demands of life" (NAMI, 2004). General consensus is that between 2.6 percentand 5.4 percent of the adult population and 5 percent and 9 percent of children constitutes the most serious end of the spectrum (NAMI, 2004). For the community this means that upwards of eight to fifteen million individuals may require extensive medical care. For those amenable to treatment (drugs, therapy, and support), 60 percent to 90 percent of individuals may experience a reduction of symptoms if properly identified (Torrey, 1997). There are many different psychological disruptions but police most commonly interact with those experiencing active episodes of depressive disorders, schizophrenia, and substance abuse related disorders.

DEPRESSIVE DISORDERS. Major depression can be found in approximately 5 percent of the population, affecting twice as many women (6.7 million) as men (3.2 million) (NAMI, 2004). It can develop at any time and affects all socio-demographic groups. Symptoms may include sadness, irritability, agitation, lack of pleasure, feelings of hopelessness, thoughts of death or suicide, and pain caused by persistent physical symptoms that do not respond to treatment (NAMI, 2004). Although everyone may feel "down" periodically or after experiencing a personal loss, but those with depressive disorders may have episodes lasting anywhere from six months to a year in duration.

Bipolar depression (alternating mania and depression) affects only 1.2 percent of the population in equal numbers of men and women. The sudden shift between the two extremes is significant: the individual going from elated and energetic to barely able to move and lethargic. Some individuals may experience rapid cycling (more so in women) where up to four episodes within a given year may occur (NAMI, 2004). Alternating episodes may last weeks or months and some individuals appear to enter a transition or "mixed" state where they exhibit symptoms of both extremes. Symptoms of mania include elation, anger, hyperactivity, poor judgment, rapid thought, and speech (NAMI, 2004). Depressive episodes have symptoms similar to major depression.

Both depression disorders require intervention and treatment, otherwise prognosis is poor and suicidal ideologies may result in 15 percent to 17 percent of patients (Torrey, 1997). Research indicates that one-quarter of police hostage-taking or barricading incidents may be attributable to depressive disorders. Often these involve domestic situations with harm occurring in 90 percent of cases (Feldman, 2001).

SCHIZOPHRENIA. Generally emerging in late adolescence, schizophrenia affects just over one percent of the population and is one of the most debilitating and costly of the mental illnesses (Flynn, 1994). Individuals may show disorganized symptoms such as difficulty speaking, thinking, or inability to follow through with activities. The suicide rate for persons suffering from schizophrenia has been estimated between 10 percent and 13 percent (Torrey 1997). The psychotic symptoms of delusions and hallucinations, which may occur only in some individuals, have become its hallmark in media presentations and the basis for community fear.

SUBSTANCE ABUSE DISORDERS. Addictions to alcohol and illicit drugs may result in drug-associated psychosis or severe interruptions in the ability to function in daily life. It is estimated that as high as 17 percent of the American population may be affected (Robins and Regier, 1991). To compound an already poor situation, research indicates that many individuals with other primary mental illnesses may engage in substance abuse further compounding their situations (Abram and Teplin, 1990). Especially in the case of persons with schizophrenia, substance abuse may further increase the risk of violence (Tengstrom, Hodgins, Grann, Langstrom, and Kullgren, 2004).

IMPLICATIONS. All of these illnesses may have inactive periods when the individual appears healthy while in structured, medicated, and supportive environments. During this time they are a threat neither to themselves nor to others. However, they may experience "active" periods when symptoms become more pronounced and severe depending on external stressors and how long the individual has been without medication. The impact of stress is extremely important as it may not only trigger attacks or active periods but escalate individuals to the point of becoming a danger to themselves and others. It is during these times that family, neighbors, or others often contact the police for help.

Economic and Social Changes Creating Pockets of Mental Illness

If conservative estimates are accurate and there are as many as eight million severely mentally-ill people in America, why are there not more secured facilities in which to treat them and protect society? The answer can be traced back to the 1950s with the conjunction of new psychiatric drugs, social change, and the fiscal realities of the post-World War II era. In 1955, the patient population of state mental hospitals was collectively 559,000 (Thompson, Rouland, and Souweine,

2003). The cost of mental health care, which ranged in both dollar amounts and quality, increased by 284 percent between 1949 and 1960 (Grob, 1994). Using the least expensive state's estimates at the time–Tennessee at $562 per patient/per year–the total cost of providing persons who are mentally ill with services in 1955 would have been over $300 million. Some states, such as Kansas, were spending as much as $2,840 a year on patients (Grob, 1994). Three-hundred million is significant even by today's standards, but truly a staggering cost in 1955.

While the costs associated with institutionalization were increasing, two other events in the mental health field began to take on momentum that would contribute to the emptying of state hospitals. The first was the development of new antipsychotic drugs with remarkable potential for treatment. Thorazine had an incredible impact on patients with schizophrenia, while iproniazid and imipramine were developed as antidepressants (Grob, 1994). This meant that lobotomies, electroconvulsive therapy, and long-term confinement might drastically be reduced by the regular administration of medications, possibly on an outpatient regimen. This philosophy was in keeping with civil liberties initiatives to reestablish the autonomy, dignity, and rights that had been previously taken away from persons who are mentally ill. Reintegration back into the community with pharmaceutical aids, although noble, was an objective with inherent problems.

The second important event was increased federal support to develop community-based treatment alternatives. The National Medical Health Act of 1946 provided the first wave of money for these initiatives. Slowly, state hospital patients began to trickle out into the community, about 50,000 individuals in the first five years. Those numbers rose exponentially with the creation of Medicaid and Medicare in 1965. In the five years following its creation, the hospital population dropped from 500,000 to just over 300,000 (Torrey, 1997). By 1994, the deinstitutionalization movement had left a mere 71,619 patients in long-term facilities and transferred 92 percent of persons who are mentally ill into the community (Torrey, 1997). The federal government took the fiscal burden away from the states and day-to-day management of persons who are mentally ill fell to the individual communities where they now lived.

The deinstitutionalization movement may have been an unmitigated progressive achievement in mental health care if not for several important points. There was a failure to understand how the federal medical programs worked and a concomitant assumption that patients in unstructured environments would continue taking their medication voluntarily. A self-defeating cycle was established when the government began to cover the cost of medications for uninstititionalized individuals. Patients who responded positively to drug therapy and were able to function within the community found that they were no longer eligible for medical drug benefits when able to "mainstream" (Isaac and Armat, 1990). Savvy individuals made sure to stay "indigent enough" to receive the assistance. Many of those who lost drug benefits after a period of successful functioning returned to their less functioning state.

This assumes that the individual even wants to take the medication at all. Some psychiatric disorders are marked by paranoia and suspicion, which discourages the sufferer from seeking assistance or taking advantage of assistance offered. Many medications used to treat mental illnesses have distressing side effects that themselves impede psychological, emotional, and physical functioning but are tolerated as a trade-off for a reduction in the more debilitating disorder symptoms. An example can be seen in schizophrenia patients who take antipsychotic medications over long periods. Tardive dyskinesia is a condition which affects 15 percent to 20 percent of those using antipsychotics and is marked by jerking, twisting, and uncontrollable facial and body movements (NAMI, 2004). Side effects can be so severe that some patients argue they were better off before the medication and given a choice might discontinue. Also associated with drug therapies is the all too common belief that once one begins to feel better medication is no longer needed. This may stem from the person's failure to recognize the chronic nature of their situation or from the euphoria of finally functioning in a "normal capacity" and feeling good. In any event, in 1995 it was estimated that potentially 2.2 million severely mentally ill individuals were not receiving any form of psychiatric treatment (Torrey, 1997).

Where are these 2.2 million people? Coinciding with deinstitutionalization was the increase in urban renewal and redevelopment. This effectively removed many of the "single- room occupancy hotels and other low rent housing" (Torrey, 1997), where indigent but medically functioning patients could find inexpensive places to live. Some were able to find other accommodations, however, many had to be redirected to shelters and still others to the streets. The end result was that many of these severely impaired individuals were relocated from hospitals to the homeless population. Estimates are that at any one time there are between 2.3 and 3.5 million homeless people in the United States (National Coalition for the Homeless, 2004), but not all homeless people are mentally ill. Nevertheless, research indicates that 25 percent to 56 percent of the homeless suffer from schizophrenia and depression disorders (Issac and Armat 1990) to varying degrees. In 2001, the U.S. Conference of Mayors estimated that the number was probably closer to "22 percent of the single adult homeless population suffer[ing] from some form of severe and persistent mental illness . . . [but] only 5%–7% . . . need to be institutionalized" (National Coalition for the Homeless, 2004). Add to these estimates the prevalence of alcohol and drug abuse among the homeless and there may be even more individuals requiring help than the 5 percent to 7 percent.

Once these individuals are on the streets their conditions may be exacerbated by illness, lack of adequate food, failure to receive medical or mental health treatment, use of alcohol or drugs, and criminal victimization. Police indicate that persons who are mentally ill are more often victims of sexual predators and significantly more likely to be victimized (Peck, 2003). Darves-Bornoz et al. (1995) found that of their female schizophrenia cases, 22 percent had been raped and nearly two-thirds of those raped multiple times. Place these mentally ill women on the street and their rates of victimization may be even greater. In a survey by Breakey et al. (1989), of homeless women in Baltimore, nearly one-third had been raped. Despite their violence, however, these types of victimizations are not the incidents that draw police attention to persons who are mentally ill on the streets. It is more often the relatively trivial "quality of life" offenses committed by persons who are mentally ill–activities such as trespassing, urinating in public, panhandling, or erratic public behaviors (Schmalleger, 2005).

Police Response to Unique Offender/Victims

Given the prevalence of mental illness in the general adult population, and the nature of a police officer's duties, it is easy to understand why police encounters are frequent. An excellent example of this can be seen in a study by LaGrange (2000) of a large metropolitan police department. Results indicated that 89 percent of officers had encountered an individual suffering from mental illness in the previous twelve-month period. This survey indicates that interactions are common. Other estimates indicate that 7 percent to 10 percent of all police contacts are linked to emotionally disturbed individuals (Borum, Deane, Steadman, and Morrissey, 1998; Janik, 1992). Officers in specific locations may have a greater number of interactions. It should also be noted that the majority of these interactions are handled without incident. Calls involving persons who are mentally ill generally are not violent but involve misdemeanor transgressions such as vagrancy, trespassing, or disturbing the peace. Research by Adams, Alpert, and Dunham (1999) indicated that 80 percent of their cases involved no force and in situations where force was used only 2 percent involved a weapon in some manner (threat or display). In the minority of cases where force is used, the individual may exhibit violent behaviors or merely be provoked more easily by attempts on the part of the officer to secure compliance thus increasing the probability of violence (Link, Andrews and Cullen, 1992). It is not an issue of blame but of failing to understand that these individuals may not respond to police interactions in rational ways.

Many of these situations are handled informally, some are referred to mental health professionals, and others end in arrest if the situation demands it (danger to self, others, gravely disabled or obviously ill). Officers encountering disordered individuals possess wide discretion in how to handle the situation, however, many feel "inadequately trained to identify and intervene" (Borum et al., 1998; 394). Although up to 88 percent of agencies provide training, the average time spent in education is approximately 6.5 hours (Hails and Borum, 2003). Based on the broad continuum of interactions, the variation of illnesses involved, the officers may have valid reasons for being apprehensive in responding to these calls. Officer frustration is amplified by the mental health care system's complexity and lack of resources, when their calls are not given priority, or when they are turned away from mental health facilities. Hospital emergency rooms in Buffalo and New York City refused half of those brought to them by police (Finn and Stalans, 2002). The individuals in police custody obviously exhibited symptoms that police identified as beyond the scope of "normal," but the hospitals would not admit them. The reasons for hospital refusal may include stringent admission requirements, or the lack of staff, equipment or specialized facilities for dangerous individuals (Way, Evans, and Banks, 1993), however these reasons are seldom conveyed to the officer. This confusion and the lack of options may contribute to an atmosphere conducive to arrest or "mercy booking" (Lamb and Weinberger, 1998; Engel and Silver, 2001).

Police officers are often assessed as successful in their duties if they can dispose of many cases quickly and efficiently. The option to arrest serves this need for "disposing of" calls involving the mentally disturbed when other options are not available or are unknown to the responding officer. Acknowledging that many officers have minimal training to aid them in identifying and responding appropriately to persons who are mentally ill, they may misinterpret behaviors as being the result of alcohol or other drugs or criminal dispositional factors. If the person's actions were "either disrespectful or too dangerous or too serious to be ignored" (Finn and Stalans, 2002, 282), they are treated in a general fashion which may result in arrest. Persons who are mentally ill are often "from poor, disadvantaged areas where rates of serious street crime and violence are high even for people who do not suffer from mental disorder" (Link et al., 1992, 277). Police who respond to calls in these areas may consider the behavior of the mentally ill person to be "typical" of all individuals.

Research indicates that those with coinciding mentally illness and substance abuse problems are three times more likely to be violent and engage in behaviors less tolerated by officers. It should not be surprising to find that 75 percent of inmates who are mentally ill also have a substance abuse problem (Consensus Project), their behavior bringing them to the attention of authorities but not perceived as abnormal. With officers reacting to outward behaviors, armed only with basic information about the nature and circumstances of the call and making assumptions based on their education and experience, we see that those who are mentally ill are arrested more than those who are not (Pandiano, Banks, Clements, and Schacht, 1999).

When officers can identify persons who are mentally ill, they will realize options other than arrest may be available (Finn and Stalans, 2002), but again this requires specialized training and knowledge. However, some of these options require significant commitments of time. If the officer is able to identify the individual as needing health care and proceeds to a local hospital, they are often left waiting by staff [an average of 4–6 hours in Memphis (Consensus Project)], while attempting admittance. This time may consume a third to a half of the officer's shift compared to the one hour to dispose of an arrest,time that could be spent on other "crime-fighting" activities (Perkins, Cordner, and Scarborough, 1999; Green, 1997). Lack of knowledge and limited time may lead an officer to determine that arrest is the fastest way to clear the call and move on to the next. Thus, persons with mental illness are transported to a temporary police holding facility until the courts can dispose of them.

The option to arrest results in a highly concentrated mentally ill population in local and county jails. Keeping in mind that the rate of *severe* mental illness in the general population is 5 percent (Kessler et al., 1999), research finds that the rate in prisons and jails to be 6 percent to 15 percent (Lamb and Weinberger, 1998). Metropolitan jails often hold more mentally ill individuals on any given day than most mental health institutions. Just as the police are ill-equipped to deal with the special needs of this population, local jails lack the personnel, facilities, and resources to provide adequate care. There is tremendous disparity in specialized services among jails across the country. Some states, such as Florida, have recently ordered screening and suicide prevention for arrested individuals suspected of being mentally ill (Borum, 1999), but these facilities struggle to meet the mandate. A survey of 1,500 jails in 1997 found that over 80 percent of facilities treated less than 10 percent of those inmates requiring specialized mental health care (Steadman and Veysey, 1997). Staffs in these facilities recognize the need for care since they are directly responsible for the protection of other inmates, staff, and the ill themselves, but resources and training are severely lacking.

One jail-based proposal recommends a screening process conducted by trained booking officers who have access to the arrestee's health and criminal files and who personally questions and evaluates using adequate diagnostic tools (Lurigio, Fallon, and Dincin, 2000). Some jurisdictions may have multiple individuals including a health care professional involved in this process, but funding restrictions typically limit the booking process to the most minimal of assessments. If a mentally ill individual has extreme needs or diversionary programs are available, the booking officer can initiate the procedures required for diverting the individual away from the criminal justice system and into the health care system. If programs are not available, officers can still employ safety measures such as suicide watch instructions or secured holding. Individuals who remain in lock-up are often provided little follow-up and no referrals to community treatment upon release (Lurigio et al., 2000; Lamb and Weinberger ,1998). The result is recidivism rates of up to 70 percent for persons who are mentally ill in some jurisdictions (Ventura, Cassel, Jacoby, and Hung, 1998). Although research indicates that individuals paroled or discharged who have support systems, transitional care, and structured environments are less likely to recidivate (Ventura et al. 1998), many persons who are mentally ill do not have or are unable to access support services and are often homeless. Thus, police officers are facing the same mentally ill individuals just weeks or months following their release.

As criminal justice and health care communities work together identifying obstacles to service and seeking solutions, creative ideas are being generated and tested across the United States. Innovative emergency response programs have been designed and implemented in larger jurisdictions such as Memphis and Knoxville, Tennessee and Birmingham, Alabama (Steadman, Deane, Borum, and Morrissey, 2000). Team members are extensively trained to understand disorders, legal requirements, and mental health care system procedures. One highly integrated program is the system-wide mental assessment response teams (SMART) seen in Los Angeles (DeCuir, 1996). Each team consists of officers and health care personnel providing teams with access to both criminal and medical histories. This more holistic approach provides a greater understanding of the needs of the individual involved and specific avenues that can be used to resolve situations in nonviolent ways. In addition, such teams have been able to liaison with hospitals to streamline admissions procedures to thirty minutes with no refusal policies in place (Cochran, Deane, and Borum, 2000), half the time of disposition by arrest. Assessment of the SMART program by Lamb, Shaner, Elliott, DeCuir, and Foltz (1995) found a significant decrease in the number of incarcerations (only 2 of 101 subjects) and recidivism was approximately 24 percent in the six-month follow-up. These results indicate that a trained, integrated approach by police and mental health care professionals may be an answer to the feelings of trepidation felt by the average police officer when faced with a mentally ill person. These specialized teams remove the responsibility for handling persons who are mentally ill from those officers lacking specialized training and education (Perez-Sheppe, 2006). Their knowledge decreases the potential for violent altercations with the police, increases the safety of jails by alternative disposition, and decreases the revolving door of recidivism response calls faced by many police officers. See Chapter 4 for a more extensive discussion of Crisis Intervention Teams. The challenge now is to find the resources to establish such teams across the country and continue the evaluative process.

REFERENCES

Abram, K. M., & Teplin, T. (1990). Co-occurring disorders among mentally ill jail detainees: Implications for public policy. *American Psychologist, 46*(10), 1036–1045.

Adams, K., Alpert, G. P., Dunham, R. G., Garner, J. H., Greenfeld, L. A., Henriquez, P. A., et al. (1999). *Use of force by police: Overview of national and local data.* Washington, DC: National Institute of Justice.

Bittner, E. (1967, Winter). Police discretion in emergency apprehension of mentally ill persons. *Social Problems, 14*(3), 278–292.

Borum, R. (1999). *Misdemeanor offenders with mental illness in Florida: Examining police response, court jurisdiction, and jail mental health services.* Tallahassee, FL: Florida Department of Children and Families.

Borum, R., Deanne, M., Steadman, H. J., & Morrissey, J. (1998). Police perspectives on responding to mentally ill people in crisis: Perceptions of program effectiveness. *Behavioral Sciences and the Law, 16,* 393–405.

Breakey, W. R., Fischer, P. J., Kramer, M., Nestadt, G., Romanoski, A. J., Ross, A., et al. (1989). Health and mental health problems of homeless men and women in Baltimore. *Journal of the American Medical Association, 262,* 1352–1357.

Cochran, S., Deane, M. W., & Borum, R. (2000). Improving police response to mentally ill people. *Psychiatric Services, 51,* 1315–1316.

Consensus Project. (2004). About the problem. Available online at www.consensusproject.org

Darves-Bornoz, J. M., Lemperiere, T., Degiovanni, A., & Gaillard, P. (1995). Sexual victimization in women with schizophrenia and bipolar disease. *Social Psychiatry and Psychiatric Epidemiology, 30,* 78–84.

DeCuir, W. (1996, October). Police response to the dangerous mentally ill. *The Police Chief,* 99–106.

Engel, R. S., & Silver, E. (2001). Policing mentally disordered suspects: A reexamination of the criminalization hypothesis. *Criminology, 39*(2), 225–252.

Feldman, T. B. (2001). Characteristics of hostage and barricading incidents:

Implications for negotiation strategies and training. *Journal of Police Crisis Negotiations, 1*(1), 3–33.

Finn, M. A., & Stalans, L. J. (2002). Police handling of the mentally ill in domestic violence situations. *Criminal Justice Behavior, 29*(3), 278–307.

Flynn, L. M. (1994). Schizophrenia from a family point of view: A social and economic perspective. In N. C. Andreason (Ed.), *Schizophrenia from mind to molecule.* Washington, DC: American Psychiatric Press. pp. 5–20.

Gillig, P., Dumaine, M., Stammer, J. W., Hillard, J. R., & Grubb, P. (1990, June). What do police officers really want from the mental health system? *Hospital and Community Psychiatry, 41,* 663–665.

Green, T. M. (1997). Police as frontline mental health workers: The decision to arrest or refer to mental health agencies. *International Journal of Law and Psychiatry, 20,* 469–486.

Grob, G. N. (1994). *The mad among us: A history of care of America's mentally ill.* New York: The Free Press.

Hails, J., & Borum, R. (2003). Police training and specialized approaches to respond to people with mental illnesses. *Crime & Delinquency, 49*(1), 52–61.

Issac, R. J., & Armat, V. C. (1990). *Madness in the streets: How psychiatry and the law abandoned the mentally ill.* New York: The Free Press.

Janik, J. (1992). Dealing with mentally ill offenders. *FBI Law Enforcement Bulletin, 61*(7), 22–26.

Kessler, R. C., Berglund, P. A., Walters, E. E., Leaf, P. J., Kouzis, A. C., Bruce, M. L., et al. (1999). A methodology for estimating the 12-month prevalence of serious mental illness. In R. W. Manderscheid & M. J. Henderson (Eds.), *Mental health United States 1999* (pp. 99–109). Rockville, MD: Center for Mental Health Services.

Kessler, R. C., McGonagle, K. A., Zhao, S., Nelson, C. B., Hughes, M., Eschleman, S., Wittchen, H., et al. (1994). Lifetime and 12-month prevalence of DSM-III-R psychiatric disorders in the United States. *Archives of General Psychology, 51,* 8–19.

Khanna, R. (2004, July 25). Case study #3: Aid call ends in mentally ill man's death. *Houston Chronicle,* p. A29.

LaGrange, T. (2000). Distinguishing between the criminal and the "crazy": Decisions to arrest in police encounters with mentally disordered. Paper presented at the American Society of Criminology. San Francisco, California, November 15–18, 2000.

Lamb, H. R., & Weinberger, L. (1998). Persons with severe mental illness in jails and prisons: A review. In J. Hails & R. Borum (Eds.), *Psychiatric Services, 49* (4), pp. 483–492, April 1998.

Lamb, H. R., Shaner, R., Elliott, D. M., DeCuir, W. J., & Foltz, J. T. (1995). Outcomes for psychiatric emergency patients seen by an outreach police-mental health team. *Psychiatric Services, 46*(12), 1267–1271.

Link, B. G., Andrews, H., & Cullen, F. T. (1992). The violent and illegal behavior of mental patients reconsidered. *America Sociological Review, 57,* 275–292.

Lurigio, A. J., Fallon, J. R., & Dincin, J. (2000). Helping the mentally ill in jails adjust to community life: A description of a postrelease ACT program and its clients.

International Journal of Offender Therapy and Comparative Criminology, 44(5), 532–548.

Nation's Voice on Mental Illness: NAMI. (2004). About mental illness. Available online at www.nami.org

National Coalition for the Homeless. (2004). Facts about the homeless. Available online at www.nationalhomeless.org

Pandiani, J. A., Banks, S. M., Clements, W., & Schacht, L. M. (1999). Elevated risk of being charged with a crime for people with a severe and persistent mental illness. *Justice Research and Policy, 2*(2), 19–36.

Peck, L.W. (2003, January/February). Law enforcement interactions with persons with mental illness. *TELEMASP Bulletin, 10*(1), 1–12.

Perez-Sheppe, A. (2006, May). Avoiding tragedy: CIT policing. *Law Enforcement Executive Forum, 6*(3), 47–55.

Perkins, E. B., Cordner, G. W., & Scarborough, K. E. (1999). Police handling of people with mental illness. In G. Gaines & G. W. Cordner (Eds.), *Policing perspectives: An anthology* (pp. 289–297). Los Angeles: Roxbury.

Robins, L. M., & Regier, D. A. (Eds.). (1991). *Psychiatric disorders in America: The epidemiological catchment area study.* New York: Free Press.

Robins, L. N., Locke, B. Z., & Regier, D. A. (1991). An overview of psychiatric disorders in America. In L. N. Robins & D. A. Regier (Ed.), *Psychiatric disorders in America: The epidemiological catchment area study* (pp. 328–366). New York: Free Press.

Schmalleger, F. (2005). *Criminal justice today* (8th ed.). Upper Saddle River, NJ: Prentice Hall.

Steadman, H. J., & Veysey, B. M. (1997). Providing services for jail inmates with mental disorders. Research in Brief, NCJ 162207. Washington DC: US Department of Justice, National Institute of Justice.

Steadman, H. D., Stainbrook, K. A., Griffin, P., Draine, J., Dupont, J., & Horey, C. (2001, February). A specialized crisis response site as a core element of police-based diversion programs. *Psychiatric Services, 52,* 219–222.

Steadman, H. J., Deane, M.W., Borum, R., Morrissey, J. P. (2000). Comparing outcomes of major models of police responses to mental health emergencies. *Psychiatric Services, 51,* 645–649.

Tengstrom, A., Hodgins, S., Grann, M., Langstrom, N., & Kullgren, G. (2004). Schizophrenia and criminal offending: The role of psychopathology and substance use disorders. **Criminal Justice and Behavior, 31**(4), 367–391.

Thompson, M., Reuland, M., & Souweine, D. (2003). Criminal justice/mental health consensus: Improving responses to people with mental illness. *Crime & Delinquency, 49*(1), 30–51.

Torrey, E. F. (1997). *Out of the shadows: Confronting America's mental illness crisis.* New York: John Wiley & Sons, Inc.

Ventura, L. A., Cassel, C. A., Jacoby, J. E., & Huang, B. (1998). Case management and recidivism of mentally ill persons released from jail. *Psychiatric Services, 49* (10), pp. 1330–1337.

Way, B. B., Evans, M. E., & Banks, S. M. (1993). An analysis of police referrals to 10 psychiatric emergency rooms. *Bulletin of the American Academy of Psychiatry and the Law, 21*(4), 389–397.

Chapter 3

NATURE OF POLICE CONTACT WITH PERSONS WITH MENTAL ILLNESS

LEONARD W. PECK, JR.

This chapter summarizes two parallel surveys from Illinois and Texas police and sheriff's departments about their interactions with citizens who are mentally ill. The Illinois survey was part of the response to a legislative mandate, Public Act 91-0837, which modified Illinois' statutes relating to taking people into custody in connection with their suspected mental illness and transporting them to inpatient care. The law also mandated a task force to consider and propose law enforcement responses to the concerns that triggered the litigation.

The initiating issue was the management of mental health warrants, which are typically executed by the sheriff's departments who use agency vehicles for the purpose. The critics noted that the use of peace officers and their vehicles for medical purposes was dehumanizing and embarrassing, especially when the patient was willing to cooperate or could be persuaded to do so. They were being treated like criminals for possibly being ill. We do not send police cars when people have appendicitis, do we? So why do we do so for persons who are mentally ill? (Same on page 16.) Ambulance staff usually has been trained in the basic fundamentals of medicine. Arguably, sheriff's departments are less informed about mental illness.

Surprisingly, given the initial rhetoric, there was a great deal of accord between the advocates and the sheriff's departments. The sheriff's department's defense was that they were doing the best they could with what they had. Especially in the less populous counties, there was inadequate demand for mental health warrants to justify either specially trained officers or special equipment. The mental health authorities were funded for treating, but not for transportation or obtaining custody. The sheriff's department's problem was one of limited budgets and resources. If their duties were to be modified, some mandate would be required, ideally one that would also affect other players in the mental health system. As noted in Chapter 1, the effort ultimately led to passage of legislation in Illinois stipulating medical transport of persons with mental illness when excessive risk exists (Public Act 093-0770).

Further, the task force quickly became aware that the issues went beyond mental health warrants and transportation, since the law enforcement system has dealings with persons who are mentally ill in every aspect of its operations. A mentally ill person can be a victim, an offender and a witness–exactly as any other person can. The survey was conducted to verify the task force's initial impressions and was sent to all Illinois sheriff's and municipal police departments that had at least 50 sworn officers. Of 88 responses, 55 were from sheriff's departments and the remainder were from municipal police departments (Illinois Law Enforcement Training and Standards Board, 2001).

The result was a recommended statewide protocol, which addressed all the ordinary contacts between peace officers and persons who are mentally ill, and the transportation of such people. The protocol also operated as the basis for training of peace officers about how to respond to contacts with persons who are mentally ill. There were model agreements for use by sheriff's departments in obtaining professional crisis intervention and training services and for formally cooperating with local mental health agencies.

The Texas survey summary was published as a *Texas Law Enforcement Management and Administrative Statistics Bulletin* (Peck, 2003). While the survey did not arise from political crisis, Texas faces similar issues as Illinois and adjusts itself to the same concerns in a variety of ways.

The Texas survey was mailed to Texas municipal police agencies with at least 50 sworn officers including a sampling of smaller agencies, and to sheriff's departments for the most populous urban counties. Thirty-five Texas police departments and six sheriff's departments responded about their interactions with citizens who are mentally ill.

Some of the differences in responses between the two states arise from the differences between the two survey populations. The Illinois survey and its responders were sheriff's departments "heavy" and drew from populous and nonpopulous counties. The Texas survey was municipal police department heavy, with a sprinkling of sheriff's departments. Moreover, the Texas sheriff's departments were selected from the larger counties, which were likely to have more demand for services and more elaborate responses to those demands. Additionally, nuanced differences between the organization of law enforcement agencies and mental health services in the two states may affect the answers to the survey in ways not apparent from the questions or the answers.

Background

"Mental illness" is a term used to describe a variety of conditions which appear to influence a person's behavior and/or how the person perceives the world. Traditional labels like "crazy" or "maniacal" fit only a small number of persons who are mentally ill and, even then, are mostly misinformed. Some mental conditions are chronic, although they may vary in intensity from time-to-time, while others are ephemeral, being obvious at one moment, and then disappearing. Some are responses to special stresses, and seem to present themselves without regard to the external environment. Persons who are mentally ill might hallucinate and see or hear things that no one else around them can, or become depressed and totally passive. On the other hand, others may become so excited that they cannot behave themselves without restraint. Most of the time, however, people who are mentally ill are legally and factually competent and are able to manage their own affairs.

Peace officers interact with mentally ill persons who may be victims, offenders, witnesses, or bystanders. Police also interact with mentally ill who need to be taken into custody or transported as part of mental health court proceedings or when they are in crisis and threatening harm to themselves and/or others. The second situation is often momentary–the citizen may be in crisis because of some external problem (e.g., marital or work-related), but his current behavior is dangerous to himself and those around him. In some cases, the crisis turns into "suicide by cop," an occurrence which is traumatic to the peace officer, those around the citizen, and obviously the citizen her/himself.

However, if citizens who are mentally ill are much the same as others, they are also different. First, persons who are mentally ill, especially when in crisis, respond differently to perceived threats. Police officers should be sensitive to those differences and act in such a way that the situation is under control and not made worse. Second, there is debate about the best way to respond to offenders who are mentally ill, consistent with public order and safety and consistent with the best interests of the offender. Advocates for persons who are mentally ill argue that these offenders should be managed outside the criminal justice system.

Public cost is one argument for wanting to divert persons who are mentally ill out of the criminal justice system. If citizens who are mentally ill can be served by the mental health system in a way that protects public safety and order that costs less than the criminal justice system, that approach is preferred. Nevertheless, diversion must be convenient if it is to work, and there must be something to which offenders who are mentally ill may be diverted.

Without a warrant, peace officers may arrest persons who are mentally ill in two situations. The first arises when a person commits an offense, regardless of whether or not mental illness exists. According to the Texas Code of Criminal Procedure, Art, 14.01(b), "A peace officer may arrest an offender without a warrant for any offense committed in his presence or within his view." According to Illinois Compiled Statutes 5/107-2(c), a peace officer may arrest a person when he/she "has reasonable grounds to believe that the person is committing or has committed an offense."

Additionally, the two states' laws provide special authority to take a person who is mentally ill into custody without a warrant when the severity of the mental illness and other factors militate for such custody. According to the Texas Health and Safety Code, Section 573.001:

> (a) A peace officer, without a warrant, may take a person into custody if the officer:
> (1) has reason to believe and does believe that:
> (A) the person is mentally ill; and
> (B) because of that mental illness there is a substantial risk of serious

harm to the person or to others unless the person is immediately restrained; and

(2) believes that there is not sufficient time to obtain a warrant before taking the person into custody.

(b) A substantial risk of serious harm to the person or others under Subsection (a)(1)(B) may be demonstrated by:

(1) the person's behavior; or

(2) evidence of severe emotional distress and deterioration in the person's mental condition to the extent that the person cannot remain at liberty.

(c) The peace officer may form the belief that the person meets the criteria for apprehension:

(1) from a representation of a credible person; or

(2) on the basis of the conduct of the apprehended person or the circumstances under which the apprehended person is found.

(d) A peace officer who takes a person into custody under Subsection (a) shall immediately transport the apprehended person to:

(1) the nearest appropriate inpatient mental health facility; or

(2) a mental health facility deemed suitable by the local mental health authority, if an appropriate inpatient mental health facility is not available.

(e) A jail or similar detention facility may not be deemed suitable except in an extreme emergency.

(f) A person detained in a jail or a nonmedical facility shall be kept separate from any person who is charged with or convicted of a crime.

The analogous Illinois statute to Illinois Compiled Statutes, 5/3-603 has much the same logic, but adds the following showings that must be made before a possible person who is mentally ill may be taken into custody without a warrant or judicial filing:

(b) In such instance the petition shall conform to the requirements of Section 3-601 and further specify that:

1. the petitioner believes, as a result of his personal observation, that the respondent is subject to involuntary admission;
2. a diligent effort was made to obtain a certificate;
3. no physician, qualified examiner, or clinical psychologist could be found who has examined or could examine the respondent; and
4. a diligent effort has been made to convince the respondent to appear voluntarily for examination by a physician, qualified examiner, or clinical psychologist, unless the petitioner reasonably believes that effort would impose a risk of harm to the respondent or others.

When is an involuntary admission appropriate in Illinois? According to Illinois Compiled Statutes, 5/1-119:

> § 1-119. "Person subject to involuntary admission" means:
>
> (1) A person with mental illness and who because of his or her illness is reasonably expected to inflict serious physical harm upon himself or herself or another in the near future which may include threatening behavior or conduct that places another individual in reasonable expectation of being harmed; or
> (2) A person with mental illness and who because of his or her illness is unable to provide for his or her basic physical needs so as to guard himself or herself from serious harm without the assistance of family or outside help.
>
> In determining whether a person meets the criteria specified in paragraph (1) or (2), the court may consider evidence of the person's repeated past pattern of specific behavior and actions related to the person's illness.

The authority to take a person who is mentally ill into custody (the two states' statutes avoid the word "arrest") because of her/his mental illness is civil and not criminal in nature and is limited to cases in which the person, without some intervention, constitutes a risk to her/himself or to someone else. The custody must be by a mental health treatment facility. Jails and detention facilities are usually not appropriate. This custody is also short-term–either the citizen is released or an appropriate court decides that he/she remain in custody and under care, a decision periodically reviewed.

The key word in both statutes is "may." A peace officer has many responses to citizen misconduct or disorder than arrest. An officer's actual response is a function of the facts, the desires of the affected parties, his own expertise and judgment, departmental policy, the practical availability of the possible responses, and community expectations.

The mental health system is composed of courts, private/governmental mental health providers, and public mental health authorities. Most mental health care is voluntary–the patient has the capacity to consent to treatment and does so. Courts become involved when there is a concern that the citizen really needs care, but either cannot or will not consent. A court may order care, but only in limited circumstances, when "there is a substantial risk of serious harm to the person or to others."

Private/governmental mental health care providers are paid by their patients, insurance, or governmental programs for which the patient is eligible. Examples include people whose health insurance covers the cost of their care, veterans, and those eligible for Medicare and Medicaid. Their services are not necessarily voluntary; a court may order mental health hospitalization by a provider who can be paid through a source for which the patient is eligible.

Public mental health authorities provide services primarily to those who are severely mentally ill and who are unable to fund the cost of their care. Mental health authorities usually act as mental retardation authorities and are typically referred to as mental health-mental retardation (MHMR) authorities. For the most part, they are the mental health care providers of last resort[1] and will usually not be involved with mentally ill citizens who are only moderately impaired or who have insurance or other coverage. However, they may be the provider of first resort in crises when the existence and availability of other providers is unknown.

Some citizens' problems are obviously and exclusively mental health matters, but many that police officers deal with are both criminal and mental. When a person with mental illness is a victim or complainant, the responding peace officer may need special skills to elicit the important information and to take proper action. When persons who are mentally ill citizen are offenders, there are a range of cases in which a peace officer may properly dispose of the matter informally, arrest the offending citizen, or transfer the citizen for mental health care. In such situations, the practical problem for the peace officer or the officer's supervisor is how to respond to the case and be available for the next call for service. Where the practical choice is between jail and mental health care, the jail is almost always available, but the mental health system is not always convenient even when it is available.

The most important decisions are made by the officer who responds to the request for service. He/she must assess the situation and identify appropriate responses. If mental health care is one of the options, the officer needs to know when a referral is available or appropriate. It is also desirable to have access to someone who can inform that judgment. In some cases, information from the citizen or her/his family or friends can turn involuntary care into a voluntary referral, but sometimes, an involuntary referral must be made and emergency mental health care initiated.

When emergency mental health care is the appropriate response, the typical first police access to the mental health system is through designated psychiatric facilities or emergency rooms. The mental health authority initially acts as the gateway to mental health care and will frequently require that other causes be ruled out before evaluation. This is not unreasonable, given that many apparent crises are due to excess drug or alcohol or more prosaic medical problems–when the substance or medical issues are resolved, the mental health problem disappears. In emergency rooms, unless there is bleeding or other obvious trauma, the medical staff will not rush to attend to a patient simply to clear him medically for psychiatric attention. An important theme in the survey responses was inconvenient access to mental health attention.

One department summarized the problem in observing that the department's typical crisis is a suicidal intoxicated person. The hospital will not take custody, and the mental health people will not screen until the citizen is sober. Since no one else will take custody, at least one officer must stay with the citizen for five to ten hours until he sobers up and is no longer suicidal. The mental health contact then becomes pro forma, with the citizen signing a form saying that he/she is no longer suicidal, told to call the mental health people should he/she become suicidal again, and then released.

This scenario presents two questions. The first is "Who should be responsible for taking care of the citizen while he waits in the hospital?" and the second question becomes "Who is actually responsible?" While the "suicidal intoxicant" described is substantially mental health-related and police intervention indisputably saved a life, it also strained limited police resources that could have been used in other ways.

This also comments on the police department's vision of its role to which this transaction is not central. This also involves a transaction in which every actor performed his duties properly as he saw them. As first responder, the police cannot morally release the citizen before he/she is safe unless someone else takes responsibility. The hospital does not claim to be equipped, authorized by law, or specially funded to take custody of citizens–particularly intoxicated persons–who are making suicidal gestures. The mental health authority is not robustly funded, these transactions do not normally occur during regular business hours, and a "drunk acting badly" is not the reason an authority is funded. In addition, all the actors endeavor to maximize their scarce resources by not taking on someone else's additional workload.

Another viewpoint is that artful responses sometimes depend on experience. Some cities are small enough that this type of transaction occurs often enough to be irritating, but not often enough to handle comfortably. They also do not happen frequently enough to develop standard responses or to obtain special funding for responding to these calls.

While peace officers are not mental health professionals, they do need some special skills if they are to be effective when dealing with mentally ill citizens, especially those in crisis. Every peace officer standards and training commission's standards mandate a specified level of training in mental health issues for all peace officers. Some departments take a more assertive view about their role and supplement the basic training requirement with special mental health staffing and training. The surveys revealed that special police staffing for mental illness was most likely to occur in large urban counties with mental health authorities eager to connect with the law enforcement community, and the law enforcement community was eager to use mental health resources and expertise.

There are a variety of ways to organize police and sheriff services for mentally ill citizens. In Texas, one approach is the Galveston County model, the first of its kind in the nation. In 1976, the Galveston County Sheriff's Office and the Gulf Coast Center–the mental health authority serving Galveston County–observed that at least some of their clients were served by both agencies. Both agreed that these citizens might more effectively be managed by the mental health providers. Two major problems were: limited mental health skills of the deputies and confidentiality duties of the two agencies. Mental health information, like other patient medical information, is confidential. Similarly, criminal justice information about citizens is not eagerly shared.

The Galveston solution was to train regular deputies in mental health care and make them employees/officers of the mental health authority who could function more effectively with mentally ill citizens. Since the deputies were in both structures, they could bridge the confidentiality gap and assure that the sheriff's department and the mental health people were not acting at cross-purposes. The mental health deputies are tasked whenever a known person comes to the dispatcher's attention, becomes a treatment problem, or a transaction appears to need their special skills (Winburn, 2003). Although none of the responding departments had explicitly adopted the Galveston model, various aspects of their operations addressed the same issues.

A related approach is the Memphis model response to a crisis. In 1987, a person suffering from mental illness was waving a knife around and threatening to kill himself when his family called the police. Upon arrival, the responding officers tried, but failed, to overpower him. Unfortunately, when he attacked the police with his knife he was fatally shot. Chaos erupted in the community over the tragic shooting of this African-American man, resulting in two changes.

First, the Memphis Police Department saturated its own ranks with Crisis Intervention Team (CIT) officers who had special training in dealing with people in crisis.[2] Approximately ten percent of Memphis officers are now CIT trained and are available whenever their skills are required. Second, new mental health resources became available. A drop-in center, locally referred to as "the Med," was opened for citizens in need of custody and mental health treatment. The facility received all patients, including those whose apparent problem was drug- or alcohol- induced.

The Memphis model produced a number of effects, including a reduction in the number of officer injuries and in the number of arrests arising from mental health calls, thereby reducing jail and judicial costs. While the Memphis model does not require officers to function as quasi mental health personnel or address liaison issues like the Galveston model, in practice many of the CIT officers have established relationships with citizens. They often are personally requested by the citizens and their families when problems arise, and a substantial proportion of those contacts avoid more difficult work later on (Borum, Deane, Steadman, and Morrissey, 1998; Vickers, 2000; Teplin et al., 2005; Saunders, 2006).

Some of the responding departments had adopted a model similar to Memphis. For example, in 2002, there were 341 certified mental health peace officers in Harris County (metropolitan Houston), Texas. The city of Houston implemented the CIT training with mental health peace officer training plus additional elements (Campbell, 2003).

Houston indicates that it has trained over 700 CIT officers and another 450 from its region. Harris County indicates that it has 150 CIT deputies. Similarly, Travis County including Austin, Texas, and surrounding counties, has committed heavily to the Memphis model.

In a follow-up interview, an officer with the Houston Police Department said that the current Houston approach (especially the deployment of CIT officers) began as a pilot study in 1999 but followed at least a decade of dialog between the Mental Health-Mental Retardation Authority of Harris County and the Harris County law enforcement community. One of the shared issues was expedited processing of mental health crises and commitments. When a mental health referral is appropriate, an officer can take a citizen to the Neuro-Psychological Center and complete the paperwork in 15 minutes. Like Memphis's Med, the Neuro-Psychological Center accommodates those whose problems appear to be drug- and alcohol-induced. Additionally, Houston has had a reduction in arrests from calls for service initially classified as mental health calls (Webb, 2003).

The Surveys

The surveys asked respondents to rank order the frequency with which their department encounters mentally ill citizens. The results are shown in Table 3.1. Community demographics, the availability of private resources for responding to mental illness, and the local context of social disorder all affect the frequency of the transactions involving persons who are mentally ill. Table 3.1 provides the rank order of reported frequency. The ranks for the two states were similar.

The survey asked about the stress and difficulty of the same types of transactions. Table 3.2 reports the predominant response for each type of transaction.

The surveys asked for the perceived likelihood, on a five-point scale ranging from much more likely to much less likely, of mentally ill citizens to be victims of different types of crimes. Table 3.3 shows that a mentally ill citizen is less likely to be a victim of homicide or motor vehicle theft, and slightly more likely to be a victim for the other listed offenses.

Agencies were also asked about special patterns of victimization for persons with mental illness. Most respondents noted no special victimization problems, and a few observed that the frequency of cases in

TABLE 3.1. FREQUENCY OF TYPES OF ENCOUNTERS.

Types of Transactions	*Mean Rank**
Family, friends or other concerned persons call the police for assistance during a psychiatric crisis.	2.66
Street encounter with a mentally ill person behaving inappropriately.	4.44
Citizens call the police because they feel threatened by unusual behavior or the mere presence of a person with mental illness	4.54
Mental ill person feels suicidal and calls the police as a cry for help	4.55
Mental ill person calls the police for assistance because imaginative threats exist	5.48
Mental health agencies or hospitals call for assistance with transport.	6.93
Mental health agencies or hospitals call for security when a client is disruptive.	7.15
Mentally ill person is the perpetrator of a crime.	7.20
Mental ill person is the victim of a crime or accident.	7.39
Court order or petition to detain, commit, or transport a person with mental illness.	7.73
Physician petition or certification to detain or transport a person with mental illness.	8.09

*Low number is high frequency. All data reported in tables is an average of Illinois and Texas respondents.

which the victim was obviously mentally ill was rather low. However, a common theme of those who did comment was that persons who are mentally ill were easy to exploit and often the victims of people they knew and trusted. Quotes characterizing the issue include:

- Persons who are mentally ill are often victimized by people they know and are unaware that they are being victimized.
- Friends and close associates tend to be suspects in thefts from mentally ill citizens.
- Caregivers are more apt to abuse or steal from victims/ Home Repair Fraud often.
- Most of these victims are not capable of being adequate witness.
- Mentally ill patients are not as acutely aware of physical danger/threats surrounding them.
- Mentally ill persons are easy victims to sexual predators, who believe victims will not understand or report offense and will not be believed if they do report.
- Homeless mentally ill are much more likely to be victimized.

TABLE 3.2. DIFFICULTY OF ENCOUNTER.

Types of Transactions	*Mean Rank*
Mentally ill person feels suicidal and calls the police as a cry for help.	1.06
Street encounter with a mentally ill person behaving inappropriately.	1.18
Family, friends or other concerned persons call the police for assistance during a psychiatric crisis.	1.28
Mentally ill person is the perpetrator of a crime.	1.31
Mentally ill person calls the police for assistance because imaginative threats exist.	1.33
Physician petition or certification to detain, or transport a person with mental illness.	1.48
Court order or petition to detain, commit, or transport a person with mental illness.	1.49
Mental health agencies or hospitals call for security when a client is disruptive.	1.57
Citizens call the police because they feel threatened by unusual behavior or the mere presence of a person with mental illness.	1.60
Mental health agencies or hospitals call for assistance with transport.	1.62
Mentally ill person is the victim of a crime or accident.	2.19

*Low number is high difficulty.
**1 = very difficult; 2 = some difficulty; 3 = relatively routine

TABLE 3.3. PERCEIVED RELATIVE LIKELIHOOD THAT MENTALLY ILL CITIZEN WILL BE A VICTIM OF SPECIFIED CRIMES.
(High numbers indicate greater likelihood)

Type of Crime	*Score*
Personal Crime Victimization	
Murder/Manslaughter	2.95
Simple Assault	2.96
Robbery	2.97
Larceny/Theft	2.99
Aggravated Assault	3.05
Sexual Assault	3.11
Household Victimization	
Motor Vehicle Theft	2.98
Burglary	3.00
Larceny	3.01
Offenses against family and children	3.06

The survey asked departments how problematic, on a five-point scale ranging from a critical problem to almost never a problem, were certain behaviors of mentally ill citizens. Although none of the behaviors were exclusive activities of persons who are mentally ill, responses varied, depending on the circumstances and the various interpretations of the question. One department might regard a behavior as problematic if it does not occur often enough, while another might regard the same behavior as nonproblematic because it happens frequently, and, of course, some departments see the behaviors as part of police work and not as problems. Table 4 shows the mean scores which ranged from 3.4 ("Somewhat problematic") to higher scores being less problematic. The most problematic behavior was threatening suicide.

Agencies were asked, "In noncustodial situations that nevertheless require longer-term intervention, who does your agency normally contact?" These would entail situations in which the responding police officer sees no need to take someone into custody but does observe a possible need for services. To whom would the citizen be referred for services? Table 3.5 reports the percentage of time departments employed each type of provider. These choices were not exclusive, leaving several possible alternatives. Most communities have visible mental health authorities (or centers–the structure of community services is in legislatively-driven flux and so is the governmental label for the community service agency).

A follow-up question asked, "In a custodial situation, to what facility are persons who are mentally ill normally transported?"

TABLE 3.4. HOW PROBLEMATIC ARE CERTAIN BEHAVIORS.
(Lower scores indicate more of a problem)

Behavior	*Score*
Threatening suicide	2.78
Physically threatening family members	2.98
Nuisance behaviors	3.03
Wandering the streets	3.34
Physically threatening other citizens	3.40
Loitering in public places	3.48
Homelessness	3.54

TABLE 3.5. PROVIDER TO WHOM NONCUSTODIAL CONTACTS MIGHT BE REFERRED.

Type of Provider	*Percentage*
Local citizen volunteers trained in intervention	1.5
Specific mental health components	4.0
Specially trained officers	11.5
Local mental health professionals (psychologist or psychiatrist)	18.5
Hospital	27.0
Community mental health center	56.0

Respondents usually selected one possible choice, although several could be indicated. The results are provided in Table 3.6.

Departments were asked to rate a set of topics in terms of training needs on the following scale: Critical training need, training very important, training definitely useful, some training might be helpful, and training unnecessary. Table 3.7 reports the mean responses. Interesting, regarding use of force training, respondents rated it at the two extremes, indicating either it was very important or not important.

A series of questions were directed to departments that operated jails or lockups. Departments were asked if jail staff always screened for the mental health of incarcerated persons. Sixty percent of the Illinois sheriff's responding always screened the mental health of incarcerated persons. The six Texas county jails and 16 police department facilities had some kind of formal screening for mental illness during booking. (Note that the sample of Illinois sheriff's was larger than the Texas sample and would have included less populous counties. Scale may be a factor here.) Next, the surveys asked about mental health screening if behavioral indicators were present. Almost 90

TABLE 3.6. TYPE OF FACILITY USED FOR TRANSFER.

Type of Facility	*Percentage*
Lockup or holding facility	4.5
State hospital	7.5
County jail	18.5
Community mental health center	26.0
Hospital	57.0

TABLE 3.7. IMPORTANCE OF TYPES OF TRAINING ABOUT MENTAL HEALTH.
(Lower scores indicate greater importance)

Type of Training	*Score*
Recognizing behaviors indicative of mental illness (including distinguishing from drug influence)	2.25
Techniques for handling specific situations (subject is hallucinating, paranoid statements, nonresponsive)	2.32
Appropriate approaches and interactive behaviors	2.42
Legal requisites pertaining to emergency detention	2.56
Use of force guidelines	2.66
Appropriate transport techniques	2.84
Custodial versus noncustodial decision criteria	2.86
Custodial procedures	2.90
Attitudes toward mental illness	3.03
Categories and characteristics of mental illness	3.05
Availability of community mental health services	3.13
Terminology associated with mental illness	3.27
Noncustodial consultation and counseling	3.40
Police role in involuntary commitment	3.73

percent of the Illinois responders would screen for mental health if it seemed reasonable to do so. The five responding Texas police departments that did not screen all inmates stated that they would contact the mental health authority. The surveys asked if the department had a provision for immediate transfer of a severely mentally ill person to a mental health facility. Fifty-six percent of the Illinois responders had provision for immediate transfer to a mental health facility. Seventy-eight percent of the Texas responders to these questions had a procedure and a designated facility for such transfers. Five of the remaining Texas departments did not have a provision for immediate transfer, but that does not necessarily mean that inmates' needs are ignored. One Texas alternative is in-jail mental health services. The Harris County Sheriff's Department stated that the Harris County MHMR Authority provided services at the jail. The Bexar County sheriff's Department responded that it had 130 employees and could handle any psychiatric emergency onsite.

Some mentally ill confinees must remain in custody. Respondents were asked if they were separated from other inmates, provided mental health services, and handled differently in any other way. Ninety-one percent of the Illinois sheriff's departments separated mentally ill confinees from other inmates. Seventy percent of the Texas departments responding to these questions said "yes", two (7%) said "no," two (7%) said that "it depends," and four did not respond to this question. Ninety-five percent of the Illinois responders provided counseling or psychiatric services. All the responding Texas counties and Texas cities provided counseling and psychiatric services. None of the other city facilities provided such services, most likely because confinees remain in their custody for short periods. Mentally ill confinees did receive some special treatment. In Illinois, 56 percent of the responders handled mentally ill offenders differently in addition to the ways already noted. Texas counties provided separate housing and mental health treatment as appropriate. Some reported that they use padded isolation cells when necessary and several of the cities reported that they expedited the transfer of mentally ill confinees to county jail.

Both surveys asked about transporting people with mental illness pursuant to court orders and petitions. Most of the preceding questions about lockups and jails assumed that persons who are mentally ill were being managed in connection with criminal law enforcement functions of the departments, but mental health is also a civil issue for sheriff's and police departments. When mentally ill citizens are taken into custody and directed to court or to a treatment or diagnostic facility, someone has to take them. Traditionally, this is a sheriff's department function, but other arrangements are possible.

Both surveys asked how frequently per month their department transports mentally ill persons in response to court orders or petitions; who else, if anyone provides such transportation; and how many officers are engaged in a transport and how long a typical transport takes? The mean Illinois responder engaged in two transportations per month in response to petitions or court orders. Some of the answers suggest that many of the transports occurred when police initiated mental health commitments and their time included arriving at the hospital and waiting for mental health screening.

In Illinois, the mean transport required 1.9 officers and took 4.2 hours. In Texas, one or two officers were involved in any single transport, depending on the patient and the agency. The briefest transport, by the Bexar County Sheriff's Department, took 45 minutes. The longest, by the El Paso County Sheriff's Department, took 48 hours. (Bexar and Travis Counties have local state mental hospitals. For El Paso, the nearest state mental hospital is several hundred miles away.) Three Illinois sheriffs reported that they had calculated costs for court-ordered transports. Of the two that provided costs, one reported $1,716 per year and the other $1,440 per year.

The survey requested additional comments. Departments expressed concerns ranging from the need and importance of training to problems in connecting the police to the mental health system, in particular, the confusion and delay involved in waiting for screening, especially for emergency mental health commitments, which almost always happen after regular hours. Others voiced opinions about reverse diversion or the movement of persons who are mentally ill back into the criminal justice system. Frustration was expressed about those who needed mental health care, but were not severe enough that a court could order treatment. One respondent observed that some offenders who are mentally ill had been released numerous times and were becoming more violent. One agency stated that reductions in city and county funding were shifting social work and emergency mental detention work to the law enforcement community and the officers were burning out. Another observed that mental health services or the homeless and those with personality disorders were not adequate.

NOTES

1. The organization of mental health authority care is more complex than this article permits. For the purposes of this article, the care of the mental authorities provide consists of mental health care provided under their aegis by their employees by private providers and other governmental providers.
2. Memphis used trainers from Galvestonwhen it started its program (Winburn, 2003).

REFERENCES

Campbell, C. (2003). *Personal communication.* Austin: Texas Commission on Law Enforcement Officer Standards and Education.

Fisher, D. (2003). *Survey respondent.* Arlington, TX: Arlington Police Department.

Illinois Law Enforcement Training and Standards Board. (2001). *Task force report: Law enforcement and mental health interaction in responding to persons with mental illness.* Springfield, IL: Author.

Peck, L. W. (2003). Law enforcement interactions with persons with mental illness. *Texas Law Enforcement Management and Administrative Statistics Program Bulletin, 10*(1), 1–12.

Saunders, M. (2006, May). The state of CIT in the state of Florida: The evolution of a multicounty and multi-jurisdictional coordination of CIT across the state of Florida. *Law Enforcement Executive Forum, 6*(3), 37–47.

Teplin, L., McClelland, A. G. M., Abram, K. M., & Weiner, D. A. (2005, August). Crime victimization in adults with severe mental illness: Comparison with the national crime victimization survey. *Archive of General Psychiatry, 62*(8), 911–921.

Vickers, B. (2000). *Memphis, Tennessee, Police Department's crisis intervention team. Bulletin from the field, practitioner perspectives.* Washington, DC: Bureau of Justice Assistance. Available online at www.ncjrs.org/txtfiles1/bja/182501.txt

Webb, F. (2003). *Survey respondent.* Houston, TX: Houston Police Department.

Winburn, M. (2003). *Personal communication.* Galveston, TX: Gulf Coast Mental Health, Mental Retardation Center.

Part II

Issues for Law Enforcement

Chapter 4

LAW ENFORCEMENT POLICY RECOMMENDATIONS

MELISSA W. REULAND

Though many law enforcement agencies have worked creatively and with genuine concern for persons with mental illness, these agencies often lack the resources and expertise to deal with the problems persons with mental illness typically experience. Their difficulties stem from a lack of academy training for new recruits that addresses unique factors associated with this population, a shortage of law enforcement response options geared toward the special needs of persons with mental illnesses, and minimal relationships between law enforcement and the mental health care community. Additionally, like the general public, some members of the law enforcement community may hold stereotypes and misconceptions about mentally ill persons, which contribute to a climate of fear and stigma. Due to these and other factors, the law enforcement response has not always met the needs of persons with mental illnesses.

In recent years, however, some law enforcement agencies have begun to build on the successes of others to create new collaborative approaches. These agencies have been prompted by a variety of factors, including decisions made by proactive law enforcement executives, entreaties of mental health advocacy communities, critical incidents, or lawsuits against the municipality. Regardless of the catalyst, there has been great progress made by a significant number of agencies in improving law enforcement's response in this area. It is critical to share these experiences so other agencies can make similar strides.

This chapter outlines a comprehensive series of policy recommendations for law enforcement agencies designed to improve their responses to persons with mental illness. The Police Executive Research Forum (PERF) developed these recommendations under the auspices of the Criminal Justice Mental Health Consensus Project.[1] PERF interview extensively approximately 30 law enforcement agencies engaged in creative new approaches. PERF also convened an advisory board to provide expert consultation on the proactive efforts of these jurisdictions. The law enforcement advisory board and PERF staff culled the best practice elements from these data, and provided policy recommendations to promote their adoption. The resulting Consensus Project report provides sections on the law enforcement policy recommendations as well as sections on collaboration, training and evaluation.[2]

We begin with a discussion of the philosophy that underlies the policy recommendations and strategies for change that can ease policy implementation–including designating a liaison with the mental health community. The sections that follow provide an overview of policies related to training and evaluation, and a review of the specific policy recommendations for law enforcement.

Strategies for Change

The recommendations for law enforcement enumerated in the Consensus Project report are supported by the philosophy of community policing. Community policing is a public and private sector organizational philosophy and management approach that facilitates community, government, and policing partnerships; collaborative problem solving; and community engagement to address the fear and causes of crime, and other quality of life issues. Agencies engaging in community-oriented policing have already committed to involving line level officers in decision-making and response processes because they recognize that these officers know their communities better than anyone else in law enforcement. The two essential strategies of community policing–partnerships with the community and problem solving–are important elements of an enhanced response to persons with mental illnesses.

An important mechanism for ensuring the ease of policy implementation in this area is to designate a liaison or coordinator to oversee such implementation and evaluation. The role of the liaison is twofold: to keep the law enforcement organizations on task and to provide a bridge between stakeholder groups and the agency. This can be a formal or informal position depending on the needs and resources of the department. However, it is imperative that the personnel in the law enforcement agency department, mental health advocacy community and local mental health resources know the liaison as the main contact. The liaison can make communication between these two systems much less daunting. This person must have decision-making authority and/or a direct line to the chief executive. Furthermore, the liaison/coordinator should be granted authority to speak for the department.

Overcoming Obstacles

Law enforcement agencies will face several obstacles when developing policies and protocols to enhance their response to persons with mental illnesses. First, almost all departments have a limited number of training dollars and time for an increasingly large number of topics. Smaller departments may be lacking personnel funds to designate a liaison/coordinator, and larger agencies may have difficulty training large numbers of officers. While it is understood that finding funding for these initiatives can be challenging, enhancing the response to persons with mental illnesses should be a priority for all law enforcement agencies. Federal and state grant programs are often available to assist in developing new programs. Additionally, the mental health community may be available to assist law enforcement with their training and response needs.

Second, while most states and the federal government have laws that provide law enforcement officers with qualified immunity from civil lawsuits if they act within the scope of their employment, an area for concern to law enforcement organizations is still that of liability. Specifically, law enforcement executives can be held liable for the failure to properly supervise and the failure to properly train officers. Liability issues also arise when considering custodial and noncustodial transport. In addition, before establishing a Memorandum of Understanding (MOU), it is recommended that the city attorney review any agreements to sort out any legal issues between the mental health provider and the law enforcement agency. Specifically, the issues of due care and police concerns regarding creating standards of care are of the utmost importance.

With all of these resource constraints and challenges in mind, the recommendations below have been designed as a road map to establishing an enhanced response to persons with mental illnesses. By no means is it suggested that these recommendations are the only method to enhance response or that improved services are guaranteed if they are followed. However, these recommendations have worked for other departments and serve as a good starting point.

Based on this knowledge, the goals of a coordinated approach to enhancing service to persons with mental illnesses include

- improved community partnerships;
- enhanced skills for sworn and civilian personnel;
- reduced injuries to officers;
- reduced injuries to persons with mental illness;
- reduced numbers of persons with mental illness incarcerated inappropriately;
- de-stigmatization of those with a mental illness; and
- facilitated access to service.

The remainder of this chapter is divided into three main sections: Policies related to training, evaluation and police response protocols. Collaboration issues are addresses later in this book (see Chapter 10). The sections on training and evaluation provide a brief overview of the Consensus Report recommendations. The section on police response protocols is more detailed, providing first an overarching recommendation for law enforcement, followed by related sub-recommendations reflecting elements of the theme. The recommendations are divided into categories based on five key points in time when law enforcement personnel must make decisions about how to respond to persons with mental illness.

Training

Although many experts agree that training is not the only part of an effective police response, they also agree that it is essential to any department's efforts to improve responses to persons with mental illnesses. In fact, training alone has been shown to make a difference in the way officers respond to persons with mental illnesses (see Chapter 7). It is also important to understand that training is not a panacea, and even with the best education and guidance, law enforcement officers may not always know what the best course of action is.

Training law enforcement personnel alone is not sufficient to make the type of changes needed in the system response to persons with mental illness. It may therefore be important for police to partner with mental health professionals to provide training to those in the mental health arena, consumers and their families, and even the public at large. For example, family members and friends of persons with mental illness should be educated about the type and amount of information they should convey to dispatchers when making a call for police service. This information is essential to make sure officers are prepared with relevant information when they arrive at the scene. Education for family members can also include information on what to do when the police arrive at the scene. For example, because officers may not know who is the subject of the call and who is the caller, the family member should be cautioned against carrying things that could be perceived as a weapon.

The Consensus Report recommendations for training policy include guidance for law enforcement in developing and implementing training curricula for their own personnel as well as guidance for training the community and mental health providers. The policies address: (1) convening a curriculum development committee, (2) training implementation logistics, (3) topics and techniques for training law enforcement personnel at all levels (full staff, new recruits, new hires, in-service patrol staff, special teams/advanced), (4) local, state and federal standards, (5) resources for training, and (6) assessing training quality.

Evaluation

Program evaluation is an integral part of any systemic reform effort. Evaluation mechanisms should be created contemporaneously with the program to be evaluated. The simultaneous development of a program and an evaluation mechanism ingrains the mechanism (client surveys, benchmarking, etc.) into the program. In addition, the systemic collection of project data allows police organizations to track progress for internal (quality management, resource allocation) and external purposes (funding, certification programs) and can provide early indications of trouble in the project.

Evaluation programs should measure program success at all levels. The evaluation mechanisms chosen should not focus exclusively on outcome measures. The organization should also gather data on the process that produces the outcome. The failure to measure satisfaction with the process may negatively impact the program. For example, evaluating outcome measures alone will not inform administrators that line staff find the reporting and follow-up procedure implemented by the administration to be cumbersome and tedious. Officers find the reporting and follow-up requirements to be tedious and unnecessary in some circumstances. A police organization that did not evaluate the process as well as the outcome might become aware of officer dissatisfaction with the process when it is too late and outcomes are affected.

Program evaluation should extend beyond the police organization, if possible. When a partnership implements a project all partners should be responsible for evaluating their work in the project. Implementing evaluation measures at each step of a project serves as an "early warning system," allowing the partnership to adjust aspects of the program before there is a negative impact. Systemic evaluation also provides the partnership and the partners with a concrete measure of the partnership's progress toward its goal and the contribution of the partners. Such information can have the added benefit of boosting confidence in the partnership and partners.

Police organizations are encouraged to be creative in creating and implementing evaluation measures. Organizations required by funding requirements to implement certain measures should go beyond those measures, and organizations without such restrictions should go beyond the standard of the measures. Organizations implementing programs to better serve persons with mental illness should consider evaluating their programs using the following indicators of success:

- advocate acceptance of the program
- consumer acceptance of the program
- number of escorts/police-initiated contacts with the mental health system
- decreased number of arrests
- level of collaboration with project partners

- scope of the partnership
- increased number of clients in the mental health system
- officer response to training on mental health
- increased number of hospitalizations
- increased number of referrals for treatment
- increased contact between law enforcement and social service providers
- increased mental health personnel
- increased social service personnel

Any police organization implementing an evaluation system should be aware of the need to protect confidential information from inadvertent disclosure. The need to protect information against disclosure is of particular concern when the project may involve the transfer of medical and/or mental health information. Police organizations should identify the information that is necessary for project implementation and evaluation in order to avoid "information overload." Police organizations concerned about inadvertent disclosures and information overload should consider removing identifiable information (name, date of birth, social security number) as part of the data collection process.

Police Response Protocols

This section reviews the information contained in the Consensus Project report involving recommendations for law enforcement response. As noted in the report, police encounter persons with mental illnesses in five general situations: (1) as a victim of a crime, (2) as a witness to a crime, (3) as the subject of a nuisance call, (4) as a possible offender, and (5) as a danger to themselves or others. It is also true that the person with a mental illness may fall into more than one category at a time. It is critical for the officer who responds to the scene to recognize whether mental illness may be a factor in the incident, and to what extent, before deciding which response is best.

Several different approaches have been developed to enable officers to effectively assess situations involving persons with mental illnesses that both reduce their contacts with the criminal justice system and ensure on-scene safety. The safety of all involved parties–the person with mental illness, family members, bystanders and police–is of paramount importance. The desired outcome of these contacts should be problem resolution that entails fair and dignified treatment of persons with mental illnesses.

The first step for law enforcement in developing protocols is to learn about successful approaches other law enforcement agencies have adopted. A group of key stakeholders should be designated as a planning group to investigate and assess the different responses so that community leaders can develop response protocols that meet the unique needs of in the community. This research and investigation can be accomplished using a variety of sources, including reviewing the literature; speaking with other law enforcement agencies about their promising approaches and any barriers to their success; or attending the training of a department that employs a response that could be effective in their community.

Approaches to consider include the following. They may be adapted to the specific needs of a community.

- *Crisis Intervention Team (CIT)*–The CIT approach employs specially trained uniformed officers to act as primary or secondary responders to every call in which mental illness is a factor. Ideally, officers are chosen to participate based on their willingness to enhance services to persons with mental illnesses within the community. CIT officers are available for each shift to provide assistance to consumers and their families, and to facilitate emergency mental health assessments.
- *Mental health professionals who co-respond*–Some law enforcement agencies hire licensed mental health workers as secondary responders. These civilians serve in units that are either located in the police department–and the civilian workers are under the supervision of the Chief–or they reside outside the department because they require shared staffing with other county or city mental health providers. These civilian workers either ride along with officers in special teams or respond when called by an officer after the scene has been secured for various crisis calls, including those involving persons with mental illnesses. The civilian employees are responsible for developing relationships with community-based organizations and finding available services within the community.

- *Comprehensive Advance Response*–This response model can be described as a traditional response modified by mandating advanced, 40-hour training for all officers within the department. Some of the departments that utilize this approach address responses to persons with mental illnesses as part of their training and responses to "special populations."
- *Mobile Crisis Team (MCT) who co-responds*–Generally, Mobile Crisis Teams are composed of civilian personnel who are licensed mental health professionals. For an effective, safe response, MCTs should act only as secondary responders who are called out once the scene has been secured by law enforcement. Law enforcement officers call MCTs if it is believed that there is a person involved who may be a danger to themselves or others, or if the person needs services. Also, in some jurisdictions, if no crime has been committed, MCTs can provide transport to a mental health facility (if it appears the person might meet the criteria for civil commitment) or other services (such as counseling or drug treatment). MCT personnel are knowledgeable about criteria for involuntary commitment, bring extensive information to the scene, and are able to provide follow-up services.

Regardless of the particular approach chosen, responding officers have a host of tasks (including recognizing signs or symptoms of mental illness and stabilizing the scene). The Consensus Project report provides policy guidance in five areas: request for police service, on-scene assessment, on-scene response, incident documentation and police response evaluation.

Request for Police Service

The first opportunity police agencies have to influence their response comes when the call comes into dispatch that a situation involving a person with mental illness needs police attention. Family members, friends, neighbors and bystanders call the police when they can no longer address the problem themselves. The policy statement and related recommendation for this area are in Table 4.1.

These recommendations stress the need for questions or other protocols to ensure that call-takers can recognize, whenever possible, that the call involves someone with a mental illness. This information is

TABLE 4.1. REQUEST FOR POLICE SERVICE.

POLICY STATEMENT: Provide dispatcher with tools to determine whether mental illness may be a factor in a call for service and to use that information to dispatch the call to the appropriate responder.

a. Provide dispatchers with questions that help determine whether mental illness is relevant to the call for service.
b. Provide dispatchers with tools that determine whether the situation involves violence or weapons.
c. Provide dispatchers with a flowchart to facilitate dispatch of the call to designated personnel.
d. Use designated codes and appropriate language when dispatching the call.

helpful for two reasons. First, it enables the dispatcher to dispatch the call to the appropriate responders, who may be someone with special training or other expertise. Second, the information can be captured in the computer-aided dispatch system to enable officers to track repeated calls to the location. A critical component of the call-takers' responsibilities is to determine whether the situation involves weapons or a person with a history of violence. Finally, the language that dispatchers use over the radio has the potential to stigmatize persons with mental illness. For example, agencies should use terms that describe the behavior observed by the caller and should avoid using derogatory or stereotypical words or phrases.

On-Scene Assessment

This policy statement and related recommendations (shown in Table 4.2) focus on helping officers ensure the safety of everyone at the scene while determining whether mental illness is a factor in the call. To accomplish this, officers must use appropriate techniques to stabilize the scene so they can look for signs of mental illness. The Consensus Project report recommends that specialized responses include consultation with someone who has expertise in mental illness, either a specially trained officer or a mental health professional that is present at the scene or available by telephone. As part of the assessment phase, the officer must also determine whether a serious crime has been committed and whether the person meets the criteria for emergency mental health evaluation.

TABLE 4.2. ON-SCENE ASSESSMENT.

POLICY STATEMENT: Develop procedures that require officers to determine whether mental illness is a factor in the incident and whether a serious crime has been committed–while ensuring the safety of all involved parties.

a. Stabilize the scene using de-escalation techniques appropriate for people with mental illnesses.
b. Recognize signs or symptoms that may indicate that mental illness is a factor in the incident.
c. Determine whether a serious crime has been committed.
d. Consult personnel with expertise in mental illness to enhance successful incident management.
e. Determine whether the person may meet the state criteria for emergency evaluation.

On-Scene Response

Once the officer determines that the person's behavior may indicate mental illness and a serious crime has not been committed, the officer must decide what response option is best. It is critical in these situations for officers to have a range of options at their disposal. This is why several recommendations in Table 4.3 relate to the provision of comprehensive mental health services. A key recommendation for law enforcement is to establish formal partnership agreements with mental health professionals who need to provide necessary services.

This section also contains two recommendations focused on victims. First, it is recommended that law enforcement agencies provide information to persons with mental illnesses who have been victimized by crime, so as to prevent re-victimization and increase their understanding of the criminal justice system. In addition, it is recommended that agencies provide information about community resources and what to expect from the criminal justice system to those who may have been victimized by a person with mental illness.

This section also addresses transportation of persons with mental illness, the guide here being with the least restrictive restraint possible, and the need for suicide screening at the police lock-up or other detention facility, even if persons suspected of having a mental illness are only there for a short time.

TABLE 4.3. ON-SCENE RESPONSE.

POLICY STATEMENT: Establish written protocols that enable officers to implement an appropriate response based on the nature of the incident, the behavior of the person with mental illness, and available resources.

a. Institute a flowchart that matches hypothetical situations with disposition options.
b. Designate area hospitals or mental health facilities as disposition centers that facilitate intake for people with mental illnesses who require emergency psychiatric evaluation.
c. Ensure that comprehensive emergency psychiatric services are available to law enforcement agencies for around-the-clock intake, 24 hours a day, 7 days a week.
d. Formalize agreements between law enforcement and mental health partners participating in protocols.
e. Ensure that mental health services and supports are available for every person in need.
f. Ensure that specially trained mental health professionals are available to respond to scenes involving barricaded or suicidal suspects.
g. Provide information to victims with mental illnesses and their families to help prevent revictimization and increase understanding or criminal justice procedures.
h. Inform affected third parties, including victims, minors, and the elderly, about what to expect and what community resources are available.
i. Disengage or transport the person to the appropriate facility with the least restrictive restraint possible.
j. Conduct suicide screening for all people with mental illnesses who are detained for short times in a police lock-up or jail.

Incident Documentation

Table 4.4 reviews the policy statement and recommendations that argue the need for documentation of incidents involving persons with mental illness, so that data can be used to determine whether people are being helped by the improved responses. This process promotes accountability for police actions and enhances police service to the public. When collecting this data–both from calls for service and incidents–departments should only document *observable* behavior and only document information related to the person's mental illness when it is *relevant* to the incident. These procedures safeguard the privacy of this health information and reduce the chances that such information will be used to the detriment of the person.

TABLE 4.4. INCIDENT DOCUMENTATION.

POLICY STATEMENT: Document police contacts with people whose mental illness was a factor in an incident accurately to promote accountability and to enhance service delivery.

a. Capture information related to mental illness consistently in calls-for-service data.
b. Collect information related to mental illness accurately in police reports and supplemental forms, focusing on observable behavior.
c. Document information relating to a person's mental illness only when that information is relevant to the incident.

Police Response Evaluation

The philosophy of community policing and problem solving compels agencies to evaluate their responses and how well they are solving problems. This evaluative approach must be applied to the police response to persons with mental illness as well if agencies want to meet their goals of diversion from the criminal justice system, reduced use of force and fewer injuries to police and others.

The policy statement and recommendations shown in Table 4.5 indicate that agencies should collaborate with their mental health partners in this evaluation process. Because of the many concerns about the privacy of health information, this recommendation specifies "evaluating rates of success" in referral not any one *individual's* success in accessing services. For example, agencies can work with the mental health partners to review their data in the aggregate, such as by comparing the number of people who came for services with the number the police referred. This process maintains the confidentiality of a person's medical information while also allowing the partners to evaluate

TABLE 4.5. POLICE RESPONSE EVALUATION.

POLICY STATEMENT: Collaborate with mental health partners to reduce subsequent contacts between people with mental illnesses and law enforcement.

a. Consult with service providers to evaluate rates of success in engaging people referred by the police.
b. Analyze police data to identify individuals who have repeat contacts with law enforcement and collaborate with mental health partners to develop long-term solutions.

whether their referral procedures are working.

The second recommendation concerns the analysis of police data only. If agencies collect appropriate information on their calls for service and incidents, they will be able to identify people who a repeatedly coming into contact with police. These individuals might benefit from a more individualized approach, one that could be developed in consultation with the mental health partners involved.

Summary

This chapter reviewed a set of policy recommendations for law enforcement aimed at enhancing the response to persons with mental illness. These recommendations are addressed in much greater detail in the Criminal Justice Mental Health Consensus Project report, which is available on line at www.consensusproject.org. The recommendations can be accomplished because they were derived from the real-world experiences of several communities around the country. They are a good starting point for discussion in a community that has decided to work together to improve the situation of persons with mental illness who are in crisis and encounter the criminal justice system.

NOTES

1. The Council of State Governments (a nonprofit, nonpartisan organization of state legislators) directed the *Criminal Justice Mental Health Consensus Project* in partnership with Police Executive Research Forum (PERF), Pretrial Services Resource Center (PSRC), the Association of State Correctional Administrators (ASCA), the National Association of State Mental Health Program Directors (NASMHPD), the Bazelon Center for Mental Health Law, The National Alliance for the Mentally Ill (NAMI) and the Center for Behavioral Health, Justice and Public Policy.
2. The report is available on-line at www.consensusproject.org. The report details a series of policy recommendations for criminal justice and mental health system stakeholders on how to improve their responses to persons with mental illnesses.

Chapter 5

REALISTIC EXPECTATIONS OF POLICE

ELIZABETH PERKINS BIEBEL
GARY W. CORDNER
KATHRYN E. SCARBOROUGH

Police handling of persons with mental illness has been a topic of great debate ever since the 1960s and 1970s, when deinstitutionalization policies went into effect (see, for example, Bittner, 1967 and Matthews, 1970). Laws have been enacted that make it hard to have persons with mental illnesses involuntarily committed to hospitals for treatment (Finn, 1989). These laws emphasize that it is not a crime to have a mental illness. Now that a person who has a mental illness must be "dangerous to themselves or others" in order to be committed, it is often difficult to get help for those who seem to need it (Pogrebin, 1986–1987).

At the present time, there are no cures for mental illness, only treatments that can alleviate some of the symptoms and help control behavior. Because (1) there is no cure for mental illness, (2) many times a person with mental illness is not aware of their illness, and (3) there is no way to force persons with mental illness into treatment unless they are considered dangerous to themselves or others, a large portion of the mentally ill population is left "on the street." This poses problems for police officers. Most of the time the problem is not persons with mental illness as serious offenders; usually crimes committed by such offenders are misdemeanors (Janik, 1992). More often, the problem lies in police officers being called to handle a person with mental illness "whose public behavior warranted some form of social intervention" (Finn and Sullivan, 1988: 1). Many times persons with mental illness come to the attention of the police because they are causing a disturbance by trespassing or loitering, or they call the police themselves for help with "imaginary" problems that are brought on by their illness. Although such problems may not seem particularly serious, they can be some of the most time-consuming matters that police are asked to handle.

A majority of any police department's patrol resources are spent handling minor crimes, disorder, and providing services (Hanewicz, Fransway, and O'Neill, 1982; Pogrebin, 1986–1987); as much as ten percent of police officers' "encounters" in such situations may involve persons with mental illness (Janik, 1992: 23). Even this statistic may underestimate the true amount of patrol officers' time spent dealing with persons with mental illness, though, because these encounters tend to use a disproportionate amount of officers' total time. Pogrebin (1986–1987: 69) found that the average length of time an officer spent on mental health calls was 74 minutes, remarkably long for noncriminal cases.

Deinstitutionalization

In the mid-1960s, deinstitutionalization policies went into effect, and the country moved toward what is referred to as "community-based treatment." Deinstitutionalization and community-based treatment were made possible by "the development of psychotropic medications, research that identified the benefits of community care, patients' rights litigation, and cost-saving incentives" (Murphy, 1986: 12).

It was hoped that psychotropic medications could effectively control the dangerous and destructive impulses of persons with mental illness. The idea was that, with their erratic behavior under control, persons with mental illness would be able to function in the community. These new medications made the hospital environment unnecessary for the majority of persons with mental illness (PERF, 1997). Patients' right litigation also persuaded states to begin passing legislation with strict criteria that a person must meet before being committed to a mental health facility involuntarily.

In 1961, research revealed that mental institutions were not treating persons with mental illnesses effectively and that, since persons with mental illnesses were not receiving the care necessary to reintegrate to their respective communities, they should be released into the community so that they could learn necessary skills with the help of a support system (PERF, 1997). Consequently, federal programs were established to assist in building and operating community mental health centers which provided mental health treatment, education, and job training to persons with mental illness.

The philosophy of community mental health is based on the postulate that a person with mental illness should not be isolated from the community because of their mental illness. The most important aspect of the community-based treatment movement was to establish networks within communities that would enable persons with mental illness to live freely in the community, rather than being locked away in a "mental ward." These networks were to consist of public and private agencies that would help persons with mental illness adapt to living in the community, and to service them with mental health care (Murphy, 1986). Unfortunately, these networks never reached their potential because of financial problems and unanticipated resistance from persons with mental illnesses (Wachholz and Mullaly, 1993).

The Police Role

Across the country, cooperative law enforcement/social service networks have been formed with the hopes of easing tensions, relieving police officers from having to deal with persons with mental illness who have not committed crimes, and providing proper care for persons with mental illness (Gillig, Dumaine, Widish Stammer, Hillard, and Grubb, 1990; Perez-Sheppe, 2006). Though such networks do not solve all of the problems that communities face in dealing with persons with mental illness, many police departments are beginning to see the benefits of working with social service workers, and vice versa. One of the most important aspects of these networks is opening the lines of communication. This enables agencies to educate one another, gain a better understanding of what the other does, and build a working relationship that not only benefits the police department and mental health workers, but also those with mental illness.

These networks include a variety of arrangements, ranging from committees of law enforcement and mental health workers that meet to discuss problems on a regular basis, to mental health workers providing 24-hour on-scene emergency assistance. Early results have shown that everyone benefits. For example, in communities that have networks, the time police officers spend dealing with persons with mental illness has dropped, there is less danger involved, and greater job satisfaction is experienced by police officers (Finn, 1989). Mental health workers in communities with networks also benefit because they spend less time evaluating unnecessary police referrals, and persons with mental illness are handled by those better equipped to deal with their needs.

Some police officers appreciate the greater involvement of mental health workers in the field, while others take a dim view of this practice. The officers who are critical of the mental health profession feel that the mental health system should be doing even more than it does. For example, Perkins (1996) found that officers felt that many of the problems they had in dealing with mental illness situations were caused by failures of other agencies, rather than their own lack of skill or knowledge. Police officers often feel that the mental health system is responsible for the majority of problems they have in dealing with persons with mental illness. Their rationale for this is that "the mental health field owns the responsibility for the breakdown in treatment for the insane–not the police. You guys broke it–you fix it" (Gillig et al., 1990: 665). One likely reason for this sentiment is that the police were excluded from the policy decisions that led to deinstitutionalization, and were never fully prepared for the impact that persons with mental illness would have on their communities (Goldstein, 1990).

Information sharing between law enforcement and mental health agencies is also pertinent. Some police officers complain that they do not receive enough information, especially case specific data, from mental health workers. Most mental health workers do not release information on patients because of confidentiality requirements. Much of the tension that exists between mental health workers and police officers centers around "the issue of confidentiality of patient information versus the needs of officers on the beat" (Gillig et al., 1990: 665). While it is obvious that mental health workers must respect the privacy of their patients, we might also examine the situation from the police officers' point of view. Officers are expected to assess the mental well-being of a person on the street without the benefit of much training or any kind of background information on the person. Lack of specific information on mentally ill persons has been found to be a primary concern of police officers (Perkins, 1996). She found that officers' views about the adequacy of their training were mixed, however. Interestingly, younger officers felt more adequately trained than their older and more experienced colleagues.

Police officer reaction to persons with mental illness depends on several different things, including department policy, training, and officer personality (Ruiz, 1993; Territo, 1983). The majority of police departments include a section of training in their academies on how to handle persons with mental illness, and some also address the issue during in-service training. However, training related to dealing with persons with mental illness averages less than four hours for police academies, and considerably less than that during in-service training (Ruiz 1993; Jurkanin and Sergevnin, 2002). This is not nearly enough time for officers to become educated about an area as complex as mental illness. Of course, police officers are not expected to become experts on mental illness. However, considering the percentage of calls that departments respond to involving individuals who are suffering from mental illness, it makes sense, at the very least, to familiarize officers with the different aspects of mental illness (Ruiz, 1993; Janik, 1992). Reflecting the pragmatic orientations of most police, though, Perkins (1996) found that patrol officers emphasized the need for more training in effectively *handling* persons with mental illness, as opposed to training to distinguish different *types* of mental illness.

Ruiz (1993) conducted research on interactions between police and persons with mental illness, and discovered that one main problem police departments have with persons with mental illness is that they lack clear policies and procedures for dealing with such persons (see also Hanewicz et al., 1982, Lurigio et al., 2006). He found that some departments have very detailed policies and procedures for officers to follow when dealing with persons with mental illness. However, other departments have policies that have not been updated since deinstitutionalization policies took effect, and many departments lack formal policies and procedures altogether.

Ruiz (1993) found that when a police department lacks specific policies and procedures on how best to deal with persons with mental illness, it leaves the decision-making up to the individual police officer, who probably has little or no understanding of mental illness. For some officers, this can be intimidating and frustrating, leading to a large number of arrests of persons with mental illness on misdemeanor offenses (Hanewicz et al., 1982). This is an unfortunate practice since individuals with mental illness will not usually receive any psychiatric treatment while in jail (Gillig et al., 1990).

Persons with mental illness are often fearful when confronted by police officers. This fear may stem from the officer's uniform, or because of an officer's intimidating attitude. This fear may cause the person with mental illness to become aggressive, or may simply make it more difficult for the person to comply with the requests and/or orders of the officer. Moreover, if an officer feels awkward dealing with a person with mental illness, he or she may try to force the person to comply with requests and commands before the person is completely aware of what is occurring. This tactic is an attempt by the officer to hurry the situation, so that he may be finished with this person who makes him uncomfortable (Ruiz, 1993).

Police officers should be aware that all persons with mental illness are not violent, though recent studies show that persons with mental illness do have a slightly higher rate of violence when being arrested than the general population. This is especially true when mental illness is mixed with substance abuse (Mulvey, 1994), but this does not mean that all persons with mental illness are violent, and in fact many have the ability to reason (Ruiz, 1993). Often, the misconceptions that police officers have about mental illness come from a lack of information about the subject.

Another problem area is the frequent lack of specific contextual information in dealing with persons with mental illness. When officers are dispatched, they are usually given limited information. For example, a call to handle a person with a mental illness will show up as an individual "disturbing the peace" or some other type of "disorder" call, or the individual may be calling to complain about a "suspicious" person or harassing communication, and sometimes no further information is given (Ruiz, 1993). Perkins (1996) found that newer officers felt that their lack of familiarity with previously identified mentally ill individuals was especially problematic, both for officer safety and for efficient handling of calls and incidents. On the other hand, if a person is pre-identified as having a mental illness, this may create problems if the officer is inadequately trained in how to respond to the mentally ill. Unfortunately, officers may approach these situations expecting to deal with an aggressive person and the situation often escalates.

If we want to destroy the myths surrounding mental illness, we would do well to educate and train police officers more effectively (Hanewicz et al., 1982; Wolf, 2006). This would enable police officers to handle calls involving persons with mental illness in a safer and more competent manner (Territo, 1983). Considering that the average citizen does not understand mental illness and all of its nuances, police officers cannot be expected to adequately understand the nature of mental illness without proper training. This will hopefully erase any personal biases that an officer has about those with mental illness (see Lester and Pickett, 1978). It should also raise their level of tolerance in dealing with "strange" behavior that may be caused by mental illness. This in turn may increase their sensitivity and ability to interact with persons with mental illnesses in a more patient and effective manner (Murphy, 1986).

Another objective should be to educate officers as to why they are called upon by citizens to deal with persons with mental illness. This is important, since a call for service involving a person with mental illness is not regarded as a "choice" call (Gillig et al., 1990; Wachholz and Mullaly, 1993). In fact, most officers consider calls dealing with persons with mental illness to be nuisances, or even frightening because of the risk involved in dealing with people who may behave in an unpredictable manner. Therefore, it would be beneficial if officers understood that citizens in the community have fears and prejudices about persons with mental illness just as they have. Further, the general public is not known for its tolerance of "bizarre" behavior by people they fear might be dangerous (Murphy, 1986).

Since the police are easy to reach, and available 24 hours a day, they are the logical choice when a citizen feels threatened by a person with an apparent mental disorder. Also, police officers have the authority to detain, arrest, and use force if necessary, and they have a legal obligation to respond to calls (Finn and Sullivan, 1988). Mental health agencies may also call upon the police for assistance in dealing with persons with mental illness. For example, if mental health officials have a patient who is violent or disruptive, or if the patient needs to be transported, the police may be called upon for help. Persons with mental illness also call the police themselves for help with "incidents" that are a result of their illness (PERF, 1997).

Critics of the way police handle persons with mental illness feel that the problem extends far beyond deinstitutionalization, stricter commitment guidelines, and a fragmented mental health system. Wachholz and Mullaly (1993: 291), for example, contend that because of our "incomplete and underdeveloped welfare state," the police are forced to deal with persons with mental illness when they are brought to their attention. This puts the police in the role of "agents of social control, and associates the mentally ill and the poor as classes of people who need to be controlled."

Community Policing

One way to reconceptualize the whole issue of police handling of persons with mental illness is to consider it within the context of community policing (Cordner, 1997). At least six elements of community policing are pertinent to this topic–broad police function, citizen input, prevention focus, geographic emphasis, community partnerships, and problem solving–as described below (adapted from PERF, 1997: 61–63).

Under a broad view of the police function, responding to persons with mental illnesses might be seen as just as much a part of "real police work" as other, more directly crime-related activities. In fact, this aspect of police work corresponds closely with five traditional objectives of policing, as follows:

- *Crime Control*–Persons with mental illness may be victims, witnesses, or perpetrators of crime. Dealing with these people well, whether as victims, witnesses, or perpetrators, is obviously important.
- *Order Maintenance*–Police often encounter persons with mental illness when other citizens call to report disorderly or disturbing behavior. In these situations, officers need to restore order–doing so is greatly aided by information and training about mental illness.
- *Fear Reduction*–Citizens often have unnecessary or uninformed fears about persons with mental illnesses. Police officers can help reduce these fears by their own actions and by educating neighbors and complainants about mental illness.

- *Aiding Those in Danger*–Persons with mental illness are sometimes taken advantage of or threatened by others out of ignorance or avarice. Police officers have a responsibility to protect all people in danger of harm, including persons with mental illness.
- *Helping Those in Need*–Persons with mental illness sometimes simply need help–they may have been abandoned by friends and family, they may have "fallen through the cracks" of society, and/or they may not be taking proper care of themselves. Police officers have a responsibility to provide help to all kinds of people who cannot help themselves, including persons with mental illness.

Citizen input, another element of COP, could assist the police greatly in determining how best to respond to persons with mental illness in their jurisdictions. Most citizens probably do not have strong views on this subject or even care very much, but some citizens and some professional groups have particular viewpoints and interests and should have input to a police department's policies and programs for dealing with persons with mental illness. These might include (1) individual persons with mental illness, (2) family members of persons with mental illness, (3) coalitions and groups of persons with mental illness, such as local chapters of the National Alliance for the Mentally Ill, (4) mental health service providers, (5) related social service providers, and (6) medical service providers.

Police departments could also adopt, as much as possible, a preventive approach to handling persons with mental illness. They could try to prevent crimes involving such people (whether as victims or perpetrators), prevent disorder caused by persons with mental illness, prevent fear of such individuals, and so on, rather than merely waiting for such conditions to occur and then applying a reactive response. Preventing such problems from occurring in the first place benefits everyone–persons with mental illness, other citizens, the community in general, and the police department.

Officers with geographically-based assignments, an element of COP, would be familiar with any chronic problems in their areas, including those related to persons with mental illness. They would know the people and the conditions involved better than officers whose assignments are less permanent. People in the community, with or without mental illness, would then recognize the officers who work in their neighborhoods and trust them to deal with problems fairly and effectively. While it is true that the overall problem of dealing with persons with mental illness is a community-wide issue, problems created by specific individuals and facilities are usually neighborhood-based and best dealt with by officers who are intimately familiar with the neighborhood and its residents.

Police officers could also develop partnerships with citizens, community groups, government agencies, and private organizations to help deal with problems related to persons with mental illness. This could be as simple and locally-based as organizing neighborhood residents to help watch out for the interests of a specific Alzheimer's patient, or as extensive as networking with mental health providers and others to improve the overall system in the jurisdiction for handling persons with mental illness. The key point is that, by developing and using such partnerships, police officers increase their chances of dealing effectively with problems surrounding persons with mental illness, *and* they relieve themselves of shouldering the entire burden of handling such problems. While handling persons with mental illness often is a police responsibility, it is not solely a police responsibility. Sometimes police need to remind other individuals and institutions of their responsibilities and then work with them to effect more viable solutions.

Finally, police officers could do more than just handle calls and incidents involving persons with mental illness–whenever possible, they could try to identify underlying conditions that, if improved, might help avoid future calls and incidents. This might involve referring individuals to service providers, looking for repeat-call locations and individuals, taking the time to educate neighbors, bringing legal pressure upon family members, or a host of other possible actions. In each situation, the best actions depend on the circumstances–sometimes the officer has to do some digging for information in order to understand the dynamics and underlying conditions of the situation. This problem-oriented approach is discussed further in the next section.

Problem-Oriented Policing

The first thing that needs to be understood is that police cannot solve the problem of mental illness–they are not neurologists, psychiatrists or pharmacists. The kinds of problems that police *may* be able to solve are crime, disorder, and service problems in the community that involve persons with mental illness as victims, offenders, or otherwise interested parties. For example, in Madison, Wisconsin, several years ago, the bizarre and sometimes offensive conduct of persons with mental illness on the streets led to city-wide concern about the problem of deinstitutionalization. The number of persons with mental illness on the streets of the city was repeatedly estimated in news accounts as being in excess of 1,000. When the problem was studied, however, it was determined that no more than 20 individuals accounted for most of the incidents, and that their behavior often resulted from failure to take prescribed medications. The local mental health service then established a program of special, intensive care for these individuals, monitoring them through a variety of arrangements including, when deemed necessary, obtaining court approval for a limited guardianship. The program has continued since then, with newly identified patients being added to the monitored group. The original problem–both the fear and the actual incidents–has been greatly reduced, and it appears that the persons with mental illness in the program have also benefited.

Problem solving, or problem-oriented policing (POP), is a method of policing in which officers search for the underlying causes and conditions that give rise to crimes, calls for service, and other incidents. When such underlying causes and conditions are identified, and once they are analyzed, officers then search for alternative solutions. A wide range of both enforcement-oriented and nonenforcement alternatives are considered, with the objective of making a long-term impact on the problem.

The traditional approach to patrol often leads to rather superficial police work–officers race from call to call, not doing very much at each one other than writing a report or demanding that people cease their disruptive behavior. Then officers jump back into their cars to wait for the next call at which they will not do very much either. After doing this kind of reactive work for a few years, many officers find it rather frustrating and not very satisfying.

The problem-solving approach offers the opportunity to have a more significant and lasting impact. When underlying problems are identified, officers take the time to create and implement solutions that are not as superficial as just writing a report or demanding that people straighten up. Sometimes these solutions lead to real and lasting improvements that give officers a sense of accomplishment and satisfaction.

It is important to explain what POP means (and does not mean) by underlying problems, causes, or conditions. For the most part, police officers cannot hope to correct the real root causes of crime and disorder–things like poverty, racism, adolescence, and mental illness. However, there may be mid-range causes and conditions that can be dealt with–things like abandoned houses, poor street lighting, badly positioned bus stops, negligent landlords, unresponsive city agencies, lax procedures at halfway houses, and so forth. These kinds of conditions are "incubators" or "generators" of crime, disorder, and calls for service. Doing something about such conditions can prevent future crimes, disorder, and calls from occurring.

Persons with mental illness may be involved in virtually any kind of problem in the community–just like any other citizen. However, there are several ways in which problems might arise that have specific connections to persons with mental illness:

- *Chronic calls involving the same individual:* as a criminal offender, a crime victim, a disorderly subject, a missing subject, and so on.
- *Repeat calls to the same location:* a residence, a public place, a group home or shelter, a treatment facility, and other establishments.
- *Community-wide issues:* how best to respond to the needs of Alzheimer patients, for example.
- *Breakdowns in the system:* poor coordination between police and mental health service providers, unnecessary jailing of persons with mental illness, conflict over judicial treatment of persons with mental illness, and so forth.
- *Internal police department problems:* inadequate training, failure of dispatchers to fully notify officers about calls involving persons with mental illness, information systems that fail to identify chronic individuals and locations, and the like.

In each of these types of situations, a problem-solving approach has the potential to significantly reduce the scope and impact of the problem. If all that officers do is to respond to calls, write reports, and scold people, however, (1) problems will not be solved, (2) underlying conditions will not be improved, (3) neither the community in general nor persons with mental illness in particular will be well served, and (4) the 911 phones will just keep on ringing.

A Problem-Oriented Illustration

The literature addressing problem-oriented policing teaches that one symptom of a problem is a high number of calls for service to the same address. These addresses are commonly called "hot spots" (Sherman, 1989; Koper, 1995). Most cities have them, though some police departments may not be aware of them. Officers can be unaware of hot spots if they do not work the same beat every day, or if those who do work the same beat every day do not communicate with those who work the beat during other shifts. Either/or, officers may be aware of some calls to the same address, but not aware of the total extent of the calls.

Finding hot spots should not be a difficult task. Officers who have them in their beats should be aware of them, even if they are not aware of the total amount of calls for service to the address. Finding out the total number of calls should be as easy as asking the police department's data system to run the address in question for all calls for a specific time period. However, calls for service data may suffer from overreporting or underreporting. An address may be subject to over-reporting if the system records more than one call for the same event. Also, in the case of locations such as hospitals, incidents are recorded that actually happened elsewhere. In the case of underreporting, a run on an address may come up incomplete if an address is not recorded in the same manner every time. For example, 530 Main Street, Woody's Tavern, may be recorded in several ways: 530 Main St., 530 Main, Main and Fifth, Woody's Bar, Woody's, and so on.

While making efforts to acquire a better understanding of the nature and scope of the problem of dealing with persons with mental illness in Lexington, Kentucky, we found that the police department did not actually use the code for "mentally ill" as a primary code. The only place that mental illness would be indicated in their calls for service records is in the comment field. This warned us that whatever the computer pulled up would only be a small percentage of the actual number of calls for service involving persons with mental illness.

The Planning and Analysis Unit of the Lexington Division of Police

TABLE 5.1. REPEAT ADDRESS DISTRIBUTION OF 609 CALLS FOR SERVICE WITH CODE FOR MENTAL ILLNESS IN THE COMMENT FIELD IN 1995.

Frequency Category	*# of Addresses*	*# of Calls*	*% of All Calls Coded Mental Illness*
1 Call	302	302	50%
2 Calls	53	106	17%
3+ Calls	17	99	16%
Imprecise Addresses	Unknown	102	17%

Department pulled all calls for service that contained the code for mentally ill in the comment field for the year 1995. When we received the report, it contained 609 calls for service that included the code for mentally ill. Table 1 shows the breakdown of how many times each address was listed on the report. Half of the addresses (50%) were listed once, and 17 percent of the addresses were listed as imprecise addresses. Imprecise addresses occur when the officer is not certain of the exact address and records the street number as an even number (e.g., 500 Main Street).

We were not convinced that this report was an accurate measure of the number of calls involving persons with mental illness. Therefore, we decided that it might be interesting to learn how many total calls for service were accounted for by the addresses with 3+ calls on the mental illness list. This list of addresses included: Eastern State Hospital, a state mental institution; the Salvation Army, which runs programs to help families in need and has dormitories for women and their children; the Hope Center, which runs programs similar to the Salvation Army except they are geared towards males; and, Good Samaritan Hospital, which has a fairly large mental health ward, including a wing for juveniles. Also on the list were three boarding homes for persons with mental illness, and ten apartment buildings.

We used these reports to analyze the types of calls for service arising at these locations. We broke the types of calls for service into several categories, the most common ones being disorder. The results of our analysis are presented below, except for five Section 8 high-rise apartment buildings. We did not include these five addresses because there were large numbers of anonymous calls for service, without specific address information, making it difficult to discern any patterns connected to mental illness-related issues.

Table 5.2 presents a description of all calls for service at the four major institutions on the list of mental illness "hot spots." The institution with the most total calls, Good Samaritan Hospital, had numerous calls in several different categories, providing a diffuse profile. Crimes, accidents, and injuries combined to represent about one-third of all calls. With the investigation category added in, we see that over one-half of the calls at the hospital are instances in which police contact victims at the hospital about crimes and accidents that almost certainly occurred elsewhere. Thus, while the hospital does have a mental health ward and some of the disorder calls undoubtedly involved persons with mental illnesses, it would not seem to be the case that the hospital's appearance on the mental illness hot spot list "revealed" an unrecognized location. Still, analysis of the 120 disorder calls at the hospital in 1995 (not undertaken for this study) might uncover a mental illness connection.

TABLE 5.2. TOTAL CALLS FOR SERVICE AT FOUR INSTITUTIONS IN 1995.

	Good Samaritan Hospital	*Hope Center*	*Salvation Army*	*Eastern State Hospital*
Personal Crime	126	14	5	2
Property Crime	31	43	28	12
Disorder	120	271	77	24
Accident/Injury	31	22	3	12
Mental/Suicide	5	11	7	1
Missing Person/ Escape	8	6	6	49
Investigation	112	16	8	7
Other	144	91	33	26
TOTALS	577	474	167	133

The Hope Center and Salvation Army present a different profile. Almost 60 percent of all calls at the Hope Center and almost 50 percent at the Salvation Army are for disorder. For these two facilities, both of which provide services for homeless and displaced people and families, appearance on the mental illness hot spot list is indicative of significant related issues and problems. These are locations that the police department might not "automatically" recognize as hot spots, particularly for problems related to mental illness.

The fourth institution, Eastern State Hospital, presents yet another profile. This facility does not produce many disorder calls, perhaps due to its medical and security expertise in patient management. However, the state hospital does produce a substantial number of missing person/escape calls. These calls indicate that a mentally ill patient has left the premises without authorization, thus creating a potential problem for the person and the larger community, rather than an immediate disturbance at the hospital itself. This illustrates a different type of hot spot–one that experiences a large number of "failures" which may lead to incidents and problems elsewhere in the community.

The three profiles identified above suggest different approaches to problem resolution. In the case of Good Samaritan Hospital, the police department would not want to discourage reports of crimes and accidents, it would not seem, but it might want to explore more efficient methods of accomplishing the resulting workload, such as telephone reporting, stationing a nonsworn report-taker at the hospital at busy times, or even entering into a partnership with hospital security staff. In the case of the Hope Center and Salvation Army, the police department might want to analyze all the disorder calls occurring at these locations with an eye toward prevention or at least better disorder management. In the case of Eastern State Hospital, a focus on escape prevention would obviously be in order.

We performed some similar analysis of the calls for service for the three group boarding homes on the list. We used slightly different categories, to accommodate the different types of calls made by a private group home. The results varied from home to home, with no single pattern.

As Table 5.3 shows, each group boarding home had a different category as their highest and second highest percentage of calls. Home 1

TABLE 5.3. TOTAL CALLS FOR SERVICE AT THREE GROUP BOARDING HOMES IN 1995.

Type of Call	*GBH-1*	*GBH-2*	*GBH-3*
Personal Crime	8	6	2
Property Crime	7	8	2
Disorder	10	6	1
Harassing/Threatening	3	8	1
Mental/Suicide	6	2	0
Missing Person	0	3	18
Investigation	1	4	6
Special Assignment/Service	0	7	19
Other	5	1	0
TOTALS	40	45	49

had disorder/noise calls (25%) as their highest number of calls and personal crimes (20%) as their second highest. Home 2 had a tie for the highest percentage with harassing/threatening (18%) and property crimes (18%). Home 3 had special assignment/service calls (39%) as their highest percentage with missing person calls (37%) as their second highest. This is surprising; one would assume since these group-boarding homes all house persons with mental illness, that they would have similar calls for service profiles. However, we found through our research that when persons with mental illness call the police for assistance, as well as when other people call the police to deal with a person with mental illness, their reasons can vary greatly.

These differing patterns between the group homes suggest that the police department would want to analyze each separately, in order to develop tailor-made responses, rather than trying to implement a uniform group-home response. It seems likely that some group homes suffer from ineffective management, while others may simply house individuals with very challenging mental illness and related problems.

At the very least, though, the department might want to take extra measures to ensure that officers responding to calls at these locations, and working the beats in which these group homes are located, receive specific information about the homes and their residents.

The variety and volume of calls found at these group homes also demonstrates the usefulness of undertaking hot spots analysis, even when, as in this case, the initial basis is only secondary codes included in a comment field. The initial analysis identified these group homes as having had several mental illness calls each, and then the expanded analysis revealed that each had 40+ total calls during the year. While 40 to 49 total calls over the space of a year may not seem like a huge amount, most addresses in any jurisdiction generate 0 to one calls per year. Thus, although these group homes really were generating a substantial number of calls and were deserving of the label "hot spots," they might not have been recognized without appropriate analysis.

As Table 5.4 shows, we analyzed the calls for service data from five apartment complexes that had been on our list of mental illness calls. All five of these apartment buildings are located in different complexes, but are all in fairly close proximity to one another. All five complexes are Section 8 housing with occupants of lower socioeconomic status. Two difficult aspects of analyzing the data for an apartment complex are that (1) addresses are usually for an entire building, rather than a single apartment, and (2) we cannot be certain exactly how many calls for service were made by a person, or concerning a person, with mental illness. Since we know we could not depend upon an officer to code a call as one involving a person with mental illness, and not every call on the reports lists a complainant name, the data is incomplete and somewhat unreliable.

As shown in Table 5.4, harassing/threatening calls were the highest or second highest percentage of calls for service in four out of five of the buildings. The second most common call was for property crimes, which was listed as the second highest percentage of calls for three out of five of the buildings, but, the most interesting aspect of the research is shown in Table 5.5.

Each of the garden apartment addresses has one known person with mental illness. From the calls for service reports we found that for four of these five addresses, the one known person with mental illness was

TABLE 5.4. TOTAL CALLS FOR SERVICE AT FIVE GARDEN APARTMENT COMPLEXES FOR 1995.

Type of Call	*A-1*	*A-2*	*A-3*	*A-4*	*A-5*
Personal Crime	1	29	0	7	0
Property Crime	3	14	12	21	7
Disorder	13	13	7	15	3
Harass/Threat	11	8	42	29	8
Mental/Suicide	3	0	1	6	0
Other	5	43	4	5	2
TOTALS	36	107	66	83	20

responsible for a significant number of the total calls for service. In addition, the one address where the one known person with mental illness was not clearly responsible for a significant number of calls had almost half (44%) of their calls with no complainant name. Therefore, we cannot rule out the possibility that this person was responsible for

TABLE 5.5. REPEAT CALLS FOR GARDEN APARTMENT COMPLEX "HOT SPOTS" IN 1995.

Address	*# of Calls on Mentally Ill Report*	*# of Calls by Known Person W/ Mental Illness*	*# of Calls W/ No Name*	*Total Number of Calls*	*% of Calls By Person W/ Mental Illness*
A-1	11	19	7	36	53%
A-2	3	8	47	107	7%
A-3	16	47	7	66	71%
A-4	6	33	13	83	40%
A-5	4	15	2	20	75%

a significant number of anonymous calls for service to that address.

As can be seen in Table 5.5, at address number 5 the known person with mental illness was responsible for 75 percent of all calls for service to that address. The types of calls this individual made varied, with burglary being the most common. At address number 3, the known person with mental illness was responsible for 71 percent of all calls for service; almost all harassing communication calls. At address number 1, the known person with mental illness was responsible for 53 percent of all calls for service. The types of calls for service that this individual made were mostly terroristic threatening and harassing communication. At address number 4, the known individual with mental illness was responsible for 40 percent of all calls for service; mostly harassing communications and theft. At address number 2, the known individual with mental illness is responsible for only seven percent of all calls for service, but as mentioned above, almost half of the calls for service to this address did not have a complainant name. This individual made mostly rape calls (6 out of 8), and according to the report, there were another four rape calls with no complainant name. As indicated, persons with mental illness who call the police do not necessarily call with the same complaints, therefore it can be difficult in trying to establish a pattern of calls for service by or about persons with mental illness.

As Table 5.5 also shows, there were a large number of calls made by these known individuals with mental illness that were not coded as mentally ill in the comment field, which was our basis for identifying these locations in the first place. For example, address number 4 had 33 calls by the known person with mental illness, yet only 6 of those calls were coded as mentally ill. Address number 3 had 47 calls for service made by a known person with mental illness and yet only 16 of them were coded as mentally ill. This can partially explain why we had such a difficult time trying to determine the scope of the problem created by persons with mental illness for the police in Lexington.

The situation in these garden apartments is illustrative of hot spots created by specific individuals. In such situations, the logical problem-oriented approach is to focus attention on these individuals. In the most familiar problem-oriented situations, such individuals are either repeat offenders or chronic victims (Spelman and Eck, 1989). Persons with mental illness, however, do not fit neatly into either of these categories. Still, identifying and then focusing on these individuals might lead to beneficial responses, such as voluntary submission to treatment or increased usage of prescription medication. In an extreme case, a police department might officially "flag" individuals who habitually make false reports, providing a lower priority response or even no response at all. This rather extreme measure could raise legal and/or public relations risks, of course, which would have to be weighed against the cost savings that reduced response would provide.

Another problem-oriented approach that might be productive in these situations is to seek help from so-called guardians or stakeholders (Spelman and Eck, 1989). These might include family members, neighbors, mental health caseworkers, employers, and/or apartment staff. The police might need to be circumspect in contacting and seeking support from some of these sources, but their assistance could relieve the police of some of the burden created by these repeat callers.

Based on this exploratory analysis, we would venture to say that hot spots analysis is applicable to the problem of dealing with persons with mental illness. There are limitations to this though. First of all, the majority of persons with mental illness who repeatedly call the police live either group boarding homes or in Section 8 apartment complexes. In apartment complexes, it is difficult to isolate the calls for service by persons with mental illness, especially if there is no complainant name, and the call is not coded as possible mentally ill. From our research, we showed that it is possible to get an idea of the amount of calls for which a known person with mental illness is responsible.

Another possible problem with the applicability of hot spots analysis to the particular problem of handling persons with mental illness is what is done with this analysis. For example, we can look at the instance of the garden apartment complex, hot spot number 3. There were 66 total calls for service for the year for that particular building, with the known person with mental illness being responsible for making 47 (71%) of those calls. Another seven calls had no complainant name. Obviously this one person is taking up an extraordinary amount of police officer time. So, we find ourselves asking the question "What should the police department do about this individual?" Well, the question should be "What *can* the police department do about this individual?" The police have very limited options in dealing with persons with mental illness. One option would be to refer this individual to treatment, but the police cannot force this person to go to treatment. They could try to involuntarily hospitalize the individual, but unless the person is dangerous to themselves or others, they will either not be admitted, or they will be released after their evaluation, and, of course arrest is not a viable option unless the person has broken the law, which they may not have. So, the police are limited in what they can do to stop the time-consuming, unnecessary calls for service by persons with mental illness.

The most promising approach would seem to be a problem-oriented one. If the police take a problem-oriented approach to each hot spot, carefully analyzing the circumstances and seeking a tailor-made response, they can arrive at reasonable responses most of the time. These might involve working with staff at such facilities as homeless shelters and group homes, or seeking other stakeholders and guardians when dealing with individual residents of private homes and apartments. While the problems created by persons with mental illness are obviously qualitatively different from those created by gangs, crack houses, or burglars, they seem no less susceptible to a problem-oriented approach.

Conclusion

Thirty years after the onset of deinstitutionalization, police handling of persons with mental illnesses remains a major concern for both the police and the community. At the level of individual incident-handling, five sets of issues seem to be most problematic and worthy of addressing:

- *Attitudes*–Many police officers and citizens continue to have misconceptions about, and irrational fears of, persons with mental illness.
- *Training*–The extent of training provided to police officers is often inadequate, and the proper mix and focus of training (understanding vs. diagnosis vs. street-level handling) continues to be debated.
- *Policies*–Many police agencies do not have precise, clear and well-understood policies and procedures to guide their officers in their responses to mental illness-related situations.

- *Communication*–Frequently, communication within police departments, as well as among the police, the medical community, and social service providers about the handling of persons with mental illnesses is inadequate.
- *Systems*–Often, systems for obtaining involuntary commitment decisions are unnecessarily slow and cumbersome, as are processes for actual commitment after decisions are made.

Improvements in any of these areas would likely lead to improved police handling of cases involving persons with mental illness. Further progress might be possible if police agencies utilize the community policing and problem-oriented policing approaches described above. These methods attempt to rectify chronic conditions, rather than merely respond better to repeated individual incidents, and they try to engage more community resources in addressing the problem. While it would be foolish to expect any miracle cures for such an endemic issue, it does seem feasible that real gains could be made, so that individuals are handled more humanely, problems are dealt with more efficiently, professional frustrations are reduced, and the community experiences less fear, less disorder, and more confidence in both the police and the mental health system.

REFERENCES

Bittner, E. (1967). Police discretion in emergency apprehension of mentally ill persons. *Social Problems, 15,* 278–292.

Cordner, G. W. (1997). Community policing: Elements and effects. In R. G. Dunham & G. P. Alpert (Eds.), *Critical issues in policing: Contemporary readings* (3rd ed.) (pp. 451–468). Prospect Heights, IL: Waveland Press.

Finn, P. (1989). Coordinating services for the mentally ill misdemeanor offender. *Social Service Review, 63*(1), 127–141.

Finn, P., & Sullivan, M. (1988). *Police response to special populations. Research in action.* Washington, DC: National Institute of Justice.

Gillig, P. M., Dumaine, M., Stammer, J. W., Hillard, J. R., & Grubb, P. (1990). What do police officers really want from the mental health system? *Hospital and Community Psychiatry, 41*(6), 663–665.

Goldstein, H. (1990). *Problem-oriented policing.* New York: McGraw-Hill.

Hanewicz, W. B., Fransway, L. M., & O'Neill, M. W. (1982). Improving the linkages between community mental health and the police. *Journal of Police Science and Administration, 10*(2), 218–223.

Janik, J. (1992, July). Dealing with mentally ill offenders. *FBI Law Enforcement Bulletin,* 22–26.

Jurkanin, T., & Sergevnin, V. (2002, November). Police training response to mental health crisis. *Law Enforcement Executive Forum, 2*(4), 97–107.

Koper, C. S. (1995). Just enough police presence: Reducing crime and disorderly behavior by optimizing patrol time in crime hot spots. *Justice Quarterly, 12*(4), 649–672.

Lester, D., & Pickett, C. (1978). Attitudes toward mental illness in police officers. *Psychological Reports, 42,* 888.

Lurigio, A., Snowden, J., & Watson, A. (2006, May). Police handling of people with mental illness. *Law Enforcement Executive Forum, 6*(3), 87–108.

Matthews, A. R. (1970). Observations on police policy and procedures for emergency detention of the mentally ill. *Journal of Criminal Law, Criminology and Police Science, 61*(2), 283–295.

Mulvey, E. P. (1994). Assessing the evidence of a link between mental illness and violence. *Hospital and Community Psychiatry, 45*(7), 663–668.

Murphy, G. R. (1986). *Improving the police response to the mentally disabled.* Washington, DC: Police Executive Research Forum.

Police Executive Research Forum. (1997). *The police response to people with mental illnesses.* Washington, DC: Author.

Perez-Sheppe, A. (2006, May). Avoiding tragedy: CIT policing. *Law Enforcement Executive Forum, 6*(3), 47–54.

Perkins, E. B. (1996). *Police handling of people with mental illness: Feasibility and ramifications of a problem-oriented approach.* Unpublished master's thesis, Eastern Kentucky University, Richmond.

Pogrebin, M. R. (1986–1987). Police responses for mental health assistance. *Psychiatric Quarterly, 58*(1), 66–73.

Ruiz, J. (1993). An interactive analysis between uniformed law enforcement officers and the mentally ill. *American Journal of Police, 12*(4), 149–177.

Sherman, L. W. (1989). Repeat calls for service: Policing the "hot spots." In D. J. Kenney (Ed.), *Police and policing: Contemporary issues* (pp. 150–165). New York: Praeger.

Spelman, W., & Eck, J. E. (1989). Sitting ducks, ravenous wolves, and helping hands: New approaches to urban policing. *Public Affairs Comment, 35*(2), 1–9.

Territo, L. (1983). Assessing police procedures in handling mentally disturbed persons. *Trial, 19,* 74–79.

Wachholz, S., & Mullaly, R. (1993). Policing the deinstitutionalized mentally ill: Toward an understanding of its function. *Crime, Law, and Social Change, 19,* 281–300.

Wolf, N. (2006, May). When simple solutions are part of the crime: The case of police and citizens with mental illness. *Law Enforcement Executive Forum, 6*(3),1–24.

Chapter 6

LEGAL AUTHORITY AND LIMITATIONS

PHILLIP M. LYONS, JR.
KAREN C. KALMBACH

Statutory authority for law enforcement officers to detain against their will persons suffering from mental illness is reviewed in Chapter 3. Legislation varies little among the states. As noted in Chapter 3, the core element for emergency involuntary commitment is dangerousness to oneself or others. Statutes typically also mandate immediate or near immediate petition to the courts, and require immediate or near immediate professional psychiatric review. This chapter reviews the case law associated with civil commitment statutes, both historically and in terms of current issues.

Historical Roots of Civil Commitment

At the time of the colonization of the Americas, the responsibility for the care of persons with mental disabilities rested largely on their families. This was true both of immigrants and indigenous peoples. The picture was bleak for those individuals who lacked a support network; rarely, a community would provide for their care. Most often, though, communities simply banished such persons who often formed roving bands of drifters. Violence by such persons resulted either in traditional criminal prosecutions or, at least, traditional criminal sanctions, as no treatment was available (Brakel, Parry, and Weiner, 1985; Deutsch, 1949; Reisner, Slobogin, and Rai, 1999, Ch. 8).

Meaningful community involvement in the care for persons with mental illness or mental retardation did not occur until shortly before the Revolutionary War. In the 1750s, Pennsylvania enacted a statute to establish a hospital that would receive sick persons who were poor–including poor mentally ill people. A couple of decades later in Virginia the first mental hospital was built. At this same time, statutes authorizing the confinement of mentally ill people were springing up throughout the former colonies. These statutes were in existence at the time the Constitution was written and ratified (Brakel, Parry, and Weiner, 1985; Deutsch, 1949; Reisner, Slobogin, and Rai, 1999, Chap. 8).

Civil Commitment Rationales and Authority[1]

In the two centuries following the initial statutory developments authorizing civil commitment, despite substantial–at times, even intense–judicial scrutiny, the ability of the state to confine or otherwise restrict the liberty of mentally disabled persons has never been seriously called into question. This is likely so because the goal of civil commitment, at least early on, was always benevolent. Civil commitment was relied upon as a way of placing poor people into poorhouses to ensure their subsistence at a minimum (Katz, 1986). Mentally disordered persons with substantial financial means were served by a different legal mechanism, guardianship, which was relied upon to secure food and shelter through appointment of a paid guardian. Slowly over time, commitment came to be used as a means of confining persons with mental illness or mental retardation, irrespective of financial resources. Similarly, guardianship has come to be relied upon either as an alternative or as an adjunct to commitment, without regard for individuals' wealth.

POLICE AND *PARENS PATRIAE* POWERS. As suggested by the preceding discussion, civil commitment and guardianship have been entwined both conceptually and practically for quite some time. Civil commitments do and always have included some guardianship features. Guardianship does and always has included some of the deprivations associated with civil commitment. This same complementary relationship that we see relative to legal mechanisms also exists relative to the legal power that drives them.

The deprivation of liberty is typically premised on and accomplished through one–or both–of two types of government authority, namely, the state's police power or the state's *parens patriae* power.

Police power commitments are generally said to be those that are based on a finding of dangerousness, whereas *parens patriae* commitments can be based on other criteria such as inability to care for oneself. Of course, it is often difficult to delineate precisely where one type of commitment ends and the other begins, just as it is difficult to determine where guardianship efforts begin and commitment efforts end. Whether through police or *parens patriae* powers, and whether through guardianship or commitment proceedings, ostensibly-benevolent paternalism is a guiding force–the state is seeking to help its charges who are believed to be unable to help themselves, in this case, due to mental disorder (theoretically, the same *parens patriae* rationale undergirds and drives the juvenile justice system.)

The state's police power essentially is the authority of the government to act in furtherance of public safety and it is one of the most important essential governmental functions. The enforcement of law and punishment of wrongdoers is, perhaps, the most familiar expression of this power. Likewise, it is the exercise of power about which there is most consensus; few people would argue that the state lacks the authority to deprive fairly convicted criminals of their liberty. However, much less agreement exists about the legitimacy of flexing the police power against persons who have not been accused, much less convicted, of crime, but rather, are suspected of having a mental disorder. This picture has become even murkier in recent years as Sexually Violent Predator Statutes have come into play resulting in commitments of convicted criminals who already have served their time and who lack the kinds of mental disorders that historically were thought to be necessary to justify commitment. The blurring of these boundaries is not trivial; because of differences in underlying motives (e.g., benevolence) and assumptions (e.g., competence, blameworthiness), deprivations of liberty premised on police powers are typically subject to greater safeguards than those premised on *parens patriae* authority.

Efforts at delineating the contours of police power commitments typically focus on the importance and meaning of "dangerousness" as a commitment criterion. This is not as straightforward as it might seem at first blush. As one of us noted elsewhere with others:

> Dangerousness is believed wrongly to be a condition, such as tuberculosis, that someone either does or does not have, and that can be detected (or "predict-

> ed," if we are speaking of violence) with a certain degree of accuracy. We have argued that dangerousness is a moral attribution that can be made with varying degrees of fairness but not accuracy. (Melton, Lyons, and Spaulding, 1998, 104)

The moral dimension of the determination stems, at least in part, from the contextual variables that are at least separate from, if not altogether independent of, the individual and his or her mental illness. The determination of dangerousness must be made relative to a particular individual within a specific community. The availability of intensive monitoring within the community, for example, may lead to a determination that an individual is nondangerous and, therefore, noncommittable, in one community, whereas that same individual would be considered dangerous and, therefore, committable, in another that lacks such supervision. Thus, dangerousness is a moral judgment arrived at not through accuracy, but rather, through varying degrees of fairness.

CONTRACT LAW. As noted above, guardianship originally was intended to facilitate management of fiscal affairs of mentally disordered persons who had wealth. Some type of guardianship, thus, arguably may be necessary for the dual purposes of protecting the person from exploitation and ensuring that those who do business with such persons will not run the risk of having those transactions voided later for lack of contractual capacity. Insofar as the provision of services to mentally disordered persons involves contracts–implied or otherwise–it is useful to construe *parens patriae* power as inclusive of the authority to authorize the treatment of those who cannot consent to such treatment themselves. To the extent that the provision of mental health and mental retardation services involves a contract, it is not surprising that *parens patriae* power also should be relied upon to authorize treatment of a person who cannot give informed consent to (i.e., freely contract for) that treatment. It is worth noting that, although a commitment or guardianship occurs, such an event does not extinguish all of the rights possessed by the subject of the proceedings, even as relates to autonomy and decision making. Even committed persons, for example, retain rights to consent to–and, by definition, refuse to consent to–treatment. Of course, as with the other liberties involved, treatment can be coerced through state intervention. Absent such intervention, however, informed consent to treatment remains a requirement. Interest in guardianship as a means of facilitating mental health treatment for people who have been committed is increasing as concern intensifies about the liability that may attach to treatment without informed consent. Some courts have held that even combining commitment with guardianship is insufficient to force some treatments without specific approval of the courts (e.g., *Rogers v. Okin,* 1979).

Substantive Due Process Considerations

Neither *parens patriae* nor police powers are without limits. Indeed, many of the limitations imposed on commitment proceedings emanate from no less a powerful source of law than the Constitution itself. The practical consequence of these limitations is the clarification of commitment criteria. In order to comply with constitutional dictates relative to substantive due process (i.e., fundamental fairness in decision making), the criteria must be reasonably related to the powers being exercised (i.e., police and/or *parens patriae*). Additionally, the criteria have to be narrowly drawn so as to limit the discretion of the decision maker. These protections serve not only to provide the prospective committee with adequate notice as to the applicable standard but also to give appellate courts a standard against which to judge the fairness of decisions reached by lower courts.

Even if the criteria for commitment are articulated with sufficient precision that they adequately restrict discretion, they nevertheless may collide with another substantive due process principle, namely, overbreadth. If the criteria at issue facilitate the commitment of persons who are not legitimately subject to this exercise of government powers (i.e., people who should not be committed), then the criteria are unacceptable on ground that they are overbroad. In making this determination, courts have looked not only at the vagueness or specificity of criteria, but also at the scope of both police and *parens patriae* powers. Determining whether criteria are overbroad, courts have had to look both at questions of vagueness, and at the scope of the police and paternalistic powers. These inquiries are related; the broader the powers, the greater the substantive coverage involved and vice versa.

THE DANGEROUSNESS CRITERION. The first issue is *dangerous persons can be treated differently.* The dangerousness criterion was described above as being the chief catalyst for contemporary discussions about civil commitment. This is so because of its heavy influence on the exercise of police power in a variety of contexts. The United States Supreme Court has reviewed five such contexts, namely: (a) civil commitment of those not involved in criminal activity, (b) civil commitment of those found not guilty by reason of insanity in criminal court, (c) preventive detention of minors who have been accused of having violated criminal law, (d) the preventive detention of adults who have been accused of having violated criminal law, and (e) the imposition of the death penalty. In the first four of these contexts, a finding of dangerousness can lead to confinement based, at least in part, on preventive detention goals. In death sentencing, dangerousness is construed as an aggravating factor that allows for the imposition of the death penalty under some state statutory schemes (e.g., Tex Code of Crim Pro. art. 37.07, (2(b)(1) (West 1981)).

In light of the previous discussion about the benevolent goals of civil commitment, it may seem odd to characterize civil commitment as a form of preventive detention. Indeed, one of the rationales for commitment and guardianship proceedings is that they facilitate the acquisition of treatment services by those who are presumed to be incapable of accessing those services on their own. Such a position, though,

> depends . . . on limiting involuntary commitment to those patients who are treatable in the setting to which they are being sent, actually providing the indicated treatment, and detaining them only long enough to accomplish the needed intervention. If any of these conditions are absent, the mental health system is in fact being used for preventive detention purpose. (Appelbaum 1988, 780)

Clearly, civil commitment occurs regardless of the committee's treatment amenability; many people are committed whose conditions cannot be treated. Thus, at least some of the motivation behind commitment is the promotion of public safety through the incapacitation of dangerous people.

O'Connor v. Donaldson (1975) was the first case wherein the United States Supreme Court addressed the dangerousness criterion as it related to civil commitment. A few key points are worth considering before seeking to generalize O'Connor.

First, this ruling left unanswered more questions about civil commitment laws in existence at that time than it answered. Second, the decision led to substantial reform in civil commitment statutes, so much so that contemporary commitment statutes and procedures bear relatively little resemblance to those considered by the Court. As a consequence of that decision, and widespread legislative reform of the 1970s, most contemporary commitment laws are so different from the law by which Kenneth Donaldson was committed that the decision in his case tells us very little about what changes in contemporary commitment laws might be permissible. Finally, later decisions by the Court have made it clear that unfairness in commitment proceedings can obtain even with a dangerousness criterion. Before turning to the holding, a brief recitation of the relevant facts is in order.

Kenneth Donaldson was involuntarily committed to the Florida State Hospital. He remained there for 15 years against his will and, from time-to-time, demanded his release from the institution, claiming he was not mentally ill. He even had opportunities to be released to be cared for by a college classmate and a halfway house. In declaring Donaldson's confinement unconstitutional, the Court held: "A State cannot constitutionally confine without more a non dangerous individual who is capable of surviving safely in freedom by himself or with the help of willing and responsible family members or friends" (1975, 576). The language, thus, suggests that a dangerous person would be committable under the circumstances even though a nondangerous person would not be. Given the apparent importance of dangerousness, it is important to know the scope of the construct.

The second issue is *dangerousness can be defined broadly. O'Connor* was followed by two cases that suggest that the definition of dangerous is wide open. *Jones v. U. S.* (1983) presented the Supreme Court with the question of the constitutionality of the commitment of a man acquitted of the crime of attempted shoplifting (of a jacket) by reason of insanity. By the time the case reached the Court, Jones had been in custody for a decade. *Jones* argued, among other things, that the crime at issue did not involve substantive dangerousness and, therefore, the commitment was improper. The Court rejected that argument and held that the states were free to define dangerousness as encompassing at least what is contained in the criminal code. The *Jones* decision largely left procedural questions unanswered and turned aside the plaintiff's argument that the ten-year period of confinement was impermissible because it was substantially longer than he would have received if he had been convicted of a crime.

In *Schall v. Martin* (1984), the Court addressed some of these issues more squarely in the context of the civil commitment of a minor. Justice Rehnquist, writing for a majority of the Court approved the practice that effectively constituted the preventive detention of juveniles detained on delinquency charges. The statute at issue was similar to those in effect at the time in all 50 states and the District of Columbia. When presented with the question of whether the commitment was "fundamentally fair," the Court said the answer hinges on a two-pronged inquiry. First, the loss of liberty associated with the commitment must be justified by the social benefit that results from the commitment. Second, unless the detention occurs in the context of a criminal conviction, that is, not a civil commitment, then the confinement cannot amount to punishment. In that particular case, the Court held that the social interests outweighed the plaintiff's liberty interests, in part, because his minority status entitled him to a diminished liberty interest in the first place as compared with that possessed by adults.

As noted above, many of the issues in *Schall* seemed to relate to the plaintiff's status as a juvenile. In *United States v. Salerno* (1987) the Court extended some of the reasoning in *Schall* to adults. In that case, it held that dangerousness could be used to justify the denial of bail to adult criminal defendants. The third issue is *dangerousness and other criteria.* As the foregoing analysis makes clear, applying the dangerousness criterion is fraught with conceptual and practical difficulties. As complicated as that is, though, it becomes more complicated when the criterion must be applied in the context of other criteria. "Dangerousness to self" is considered by some to be a particular instance of the dangerousness criterion. Still others, though, consider it to be a separate criterion. Sometimes formulated as "passive dangerousness," dangerousness to self or inability to care for oneself is often used as a commitment criterion. Of course, as with all commitment contexts, the dangerousness to self or inability to care for oneself must be the result of a mental disorder. Some jurisdictions take a more proactive stance and authorize commitment where there has been a significant deterioration in functioning even if it has not yet risen to the level of rendering one passively dangerous. The reasoning for these statutes is heavily weighted in the direction of *parens patriae* rationales; the statutes seek to intervene with help before the deleterious effects of the disorder become too pronounced.

Although the foregoing standards are important and must be satisfied for civil commitment, they are not the only criteria that must be met. Regardless of the reason that commitment is sought–whether it be dangerousness, inability to care for oneself, or serious deterioration–most civil commitment statutes require additional criteria also be met simultaneously (conjunctively). Specifically, as noted above, there must be evidence of a mental disorder or disability. In some jurisdictions there must also be evidence of treatment need, treatment amenability, and/or an inability or unwillingness to give informed consent to proposed treatment options.

In addition to the critical conjunctive and disjunctive criteria outlined, there are also somewhat less substantive requirements that must also be considered either in conjunction with, or as an alternative to, the dangerousness standard. These criteria are considered to be less substantive as they tend to focus more on *how* someone is to be committed, rather than *who* can be committed.

The "least restrictive alternative" is another common commitment criterion that is also less substantive and more of a procedural safeguard. It calls for the court to be apprised of all available less restrictive alternatives to institutional confinement before authorizing commitment of an individual. It does not, however, define or restrict who may be committed.

Right to Treatment

In *O'Connor,* the opinion appears to evade deliberately the more difficult issue of Donaldson's right to treatment. Quite possibly the Court's rationale may have been that as O'Connor did not have the right to treat Donaldson, he could not have had a duty to treat him, thus making treatment a moot point. Similarly, the Court did not address whether the commitment of a nondangerous person might be justified by the provision of treatment as Donaldson did not receive treatment.

The use of the phrase "without more" (1975, 576) in the Court's opinion, and the fact that Donaldson received no treatment from the hospital (in part due to respect for his religious convictions), left open the possibility that the provision of needed services might justify the commitment of nondangerous persons for purposes of treatment alone. However, the opinion in total, complete with Chief Justice Burger's concurring opinion is clear in its rejection of the Fifth Circuit's position that the provision of necessary treatment justifies the commitment of nondangerous persons.

The Supreme Court took a firm stance on the unacceptability of committing individuals who are simply "physically unattractive or socially eccentric" (575). Mental illness or disability does not, per se, "disqualify a person from preferring his home to the comforts of an institution" (575). Nonetheless, there are a number of circumstances under which nondangerous persons have mental disorders whose symptoms amount to more than mere "eccentricity," and for whom hospitalization may be the only means of survival. Such circumstances were not addressed in *O'Connor.*

In drafting *O'Connor,* the Court allowed state legislatures the latitude to create commitment statutes which, while avoiding vagueness and overbroad inclusion criteria, focused on treatment need, emphasizing the provision of services, at the same time downplaying or ignoring dangerousness criteria.

The Least Restrictive Alternative Criterion

As revealed by case law tracking commitment legislation, the problem of vagueness in definitional criteria is challenging. In particular, how do courts delineate the point at which self-neglect becomes an inability to care for self or dangerousness to self and/or others? Considering two criteria in tandem–inability to care for self and least restrictive alternatives–helps to clarify the issue and assist in decision-making. The least restrictive alternative requires that no other remediation short of commitment be available to negate the ill effects of possible self-harm. In other words, in the case of an individual who is no longer able to care for him or herself, it must be shown that there are no other available alternatives to care which impose less restriction upon freedom and autonomy as would commitment.

Although this approach helps to define, clarify, and restrict *parens patriae* criteria necessary for commitment, it does not specify or help quantify the amount or nature of the harm sufficient to justify commitment. The typical formulation of the least restrictive alternative criterion leaves unanswered the questions surrounding what other forms of treatment must be considered and how degrees of restrictiveness should be measured or conceptualized.

The modern day least restrictive criterion is anchored in First Amendment jurisprudence. In *O'Connor* Justice Potter Stewart cited the decision in *Shelton v. Tucker* (1960) reversing a requirement that public employees report all organizational memberships because there existed less drastic alternatives to this option. Relying on this reasoning, Justice Stewart notes: "while the State may arguably confine a person to save him from harm, incarceration is rarely if ever a necessary condition for raising the living standards of those capable of surviving safely in freedom, on their own or with the help of family or friends" (1975, 575). Implicit in the O'Connor ruling is a fundamental premise that the state may restrict an individual's liberty only when there are no lesser restrictive options available to prevent harm of self and/or others.

This newly-crafted least restrictive principle was soon widely adopted by states and incorporated into revised commitment codes. Some statutes simply required that a person be judged not "capable of surviving safely in freedom, on [his] own, or with the help of family or friends" (1975, 575; see also, *Thomas S. v. Flaherty*, 1988). Although we have attempted to make a distinction between procedural and substantive elements of the commitment process, it is sometimes not very useful to separate these goals or criteria. As can be seen, the least restrictive alternative standard is an example of one such element.

Conclusion

Police authority to intervene by emergency involuntary commitment of a person suffering from severe mental illness is premised upon dual consideration of *police* and *parens patriae* powers of the state. Such intervention is first closely circumscribed by statute, and further limited by case law. The dangerousness criterion is paramount in all discussion of legal authority and limitations. Despite the specificity of statutes, and despite carefully drawn case law, a judgment of dangerousness is still a subjective one, dependent as much upon the "common sense" of individual police officers as anything.

ENDNOTES

1. The following sections are based largely on Melton, Lyons, & Spaulding, 1998, Chapters 3 & 4.

REFERENCES

Appelbaum, P. S. (1988). The new preventive detention: Psychiatry's problem of responsibility for the control of violence. *American Journal of Psychology, 413,* 779–785.

Brakel, S. J., Parry, J., & Weiner, B. A. (1985). The mentally disabled and the law. *Chicago: American Bar Foundation.*

Deutsch, A. (1949). *The mentally ill in America: A history of their care and treatment in colonial times* (2nd ed.) New York: Columbia University Press.

Jones v. U.S., 463 U.S. 354 (1983).

Katz, M. M. (1986). *In the shadow of the poorhouse: A social history of welfare in America.* New York: Basic Books.

Melton, G. B., Lyons, P. M., & Spalding, W. J. (1998). *No place to go: The commitment of minors.* Lincoln: University of Nebraska Press.

O'Connor v. Donaldson, 422 U.S. 563 (1975), vacating and remanding *Donaldson v. O'Connor,* 493 F.2d 507 (5th Cir. 1974).

Reisner, R., Slobogin, S., & Rai, A. (1999). *Law and the mental health system: Civil and criminal aspects* (3rd ed.). St. Paul, MN: West.

Rogers v. Orkin, 478 F. Supp. 1342 (D. Mass. 1979).

Schall v. Martin, 467 U.S. 253 (1984).

Shelton v. Tucker, 364 U.S. 479 (1960).

Texas Code of Criminal Procedure, Article 37.07, 2(b) (1) (West, 1981).

Thomas S. v. Flaherty, 699 F. Supp. 1178 (W.D.N.C. 1988).

United States v. Salerno, 481 U.S. 739 (1987).

Part III

Successful Police Responses

Chapter 7

LAW ENFORCEMENT TRAINING MODELS

THOMAS J. JURKANIN
VLADIMIR A. SERGEVNIN

On Wednesday evening of March 1, 2007 a family from Humboldt Park in Chicago called police because their 21-year-old grandson, who suffered from schizophrenia and was not taking medication, was out of control and they would like to get him to a hospital. In several moments of police arrival he died of multiple wounds after Chicago police shot him when he threatened officers with a knife (*Chicago Tribune,* March 3, 2007). The need for training for police officers in dealing with persons with mental illness has never been more acute than it is today (Wells and Schafer, 2006). Deinstitutionalization has brought never-before encountered challenges to law enforcement. The continually overwhelmed community-based mental health care system has placed officers on the frontlines in dealing with citizens in psychiatric crisis. The news media frequently portrays law enforcement officers as insensitive to persons with mental health problems, particularly in association with incidents whenever officers use force. Additionally, law enforcement agencies are facing lawsuits alleging mistreatment brought by persons with mental illness. Even so, there has been limited literature on the training of law enforcement officers during engagement with persons with mental illness (Vermette, Pinals, and Appelbaum, 2005; Keram, 2005; Teller, Munetz, Gil, and Ritter, 2006; Price and Pinals, 2006).

Both the mental health and criminal justice communities recognize the need for law enforcement officers to receive training designed to

(1) help officers identify mental illness, (2) improve their engagement skills in crisis management, risk assessment particularly to avoid necessary use of physical force, and (3) instruct them on how to better access available mental health resources. Less recognized is the fact that the development of such models also generates articulation of principles and strategies, and stimulates research on ways to improve intervention. However, law enforcement training in mental health intervention is still a new, developing field.

This chapter reviews the primary approaches to training law enforcement officers when dealing with persons suffering from mental illness. Some common difficulties encountered by police officers are identified and basic goals and strategies for addressing these difficulties discussed. The provision of mental health training to law enforcement officers through collaborative approaches with the active participation of mental health agencies, consumers and communities is the first step in taking training to the next level. The training process can help various social institutions to learn more about one another and can also serve as a starting point for making collaborative contacts and exchanging ideas.

Scope of Training

The importance of mental health training for law enforcement officers, along with other proactive and reactive measures such as mobile crisis teams and enhanced use of force protocols, is emphasized in the literature on police training (Borum, 2000; Lamb, Weinberger, DeCuir, 2002) The scope and quality of such training is less frequently addressed. However, for the past (almost) fifty years, researchers have been growing increasingly concerned about the inadequacy of traditional training. One of the first attempts, in 1960, of dealing with mentally ill individuals focused on training as a means to change the attitudes of law enforcement officers (Consent Decree, 2002). This was a reaction to the widespread notion that most law enforcement officers tend to be biased and prejudiced against persons with mental illness. The training strategy was intended to raise the awareness of officers to the needs of such persons.

Education and training programs, which would apply principles of serving people with special needs, were perceived as key strategies in developing a professional force within law enforcement. Roberts

(1976) examined the history of police as social workers and suggested that police officers needed training in human relations and mental hygiene; they needed sensitivity training, and they needed to know how to recognize personality disorders. According to Roberts, officers needed training so that they could provide immediate crisis intervention during emergencies and when other professionals were not available.

Training programs focusing on mentally dysfunctional members of the community have been primarily identified as cultural-awareness and sensitivity courses. Since the early 1980s, police departments that had employed the Crisis Intervention Team (CIT) approach have been stressing the importance of educating *all* members of the organization–administrators, desk sergeants, line officers and especially telecommunicators.

Since the late 1990s, there has been a dramatic increase in the range of programs and courses developed by public and private agencies (including law enforcement departments) to address issues of mental health awareness. Two national studies of medium to large law enforcement agencies in 1996 and 1999 found that from 88 percent to almost all provided some type of training to handle interactions with mentally ill persons (Deane et al., 1999; Hails and Borum, 2003). Interested readers can obtain course information from their Peace Officer Standards and Training Commissions in every state. Even so, despite all the efforts, fewer than 10% of the law enforcement officers around the nation receive special training on how to deal with people in psychiatric crisis (Borum, 2000; Jamieson and Wilson, 2000). According to Boles, Wolfe, and Fulton (2001), for example, 85 percent of law enforcement officers in California do not have adequate knowledge about persons with mental illness. Another recent study indicated that more than 60 percent of police officers had not received sufficient training to deal with people in mental health crisis (Norris and Cooke, 2000). At the same time police officers are interested in receiving training about interacting with people in mental health crisis. According to Vermette, Pinals and Appelbaum (2005) over 90 percent of police officers reported that this type of training was fairly or very important, and 68 percent preferred annual training (Vermette, Pinals, Appelbaum, 2005). As a result of this inadequacy, there has been continual demand from local governments, law enforcement and mental health agencies to improve interaction, through training, between police and persons with mental illness.

Internationally, police forces throughout the world are facing the same problems. Awareness training has been identified as particularly lacking during the training of British police officers, with only 35 percent of training programs offering the kind of training that focuses on persons with mental illness. The record is possibly even worse in terms of more specific training. In the case of joint training of police officers and social workers in the subject of intellectual ability, Bailey, Barr and Bunting (2000) found that only four police forces in England, Wales and Northern Ireland reported that they held training courses for investigators, despite the fact that twenty-one departments were conducting joint investigative interviews with adult victims of abuse who were intellectually disabled (Bailey, Barr, Bunting, 2001). According to Fry, O'Riordan and Geanellos (2002, Sydney), Australian police feel totally unprepared to deal with suicidal and mentally disturbed people.

In the United States, the literature indicates that most states provide some training to officers on how to deal with mentally ill individuals. The literature does not, however, describe the standards, quality or effectiveness of that training. Further analysis is needed in order to determine whether or not the training is adequate to meet community needs.

Multilevel and multidisciplinary training should be given to law enforcement personnel. Without proper training, police will continue to be placed in untenable situations without the proper knowledge or support they need to deal with such crises.

Current Approaches to Training

The initial mostly educational approach of the 1960s and 1970s in training for law enforcement officers to deal with mentally ill individuals (Walsh and Witte, 1975; Teese and Wormer, 1975) have been changed during the 1990s with incorporation of a more specialized focus on Crisis Intervention Teams, based on the experience of the Memphis Police Department. There are several areas of current approaches that must be examined separately.

RECRUIT TRAINING. Police recruits are introduced to the problem of dealing with persons with mental illness in virtually all preservice training institutions. The length of training varies from state to state. Murphy (1986) pointed out that police recruits receive an average of only 4.3 hours of mental health training. According to Hails and Borum (2003) among 70 medium and large law enforcement departments in California the amount of training focused on dealing with mental health crisis varied widely from none to 41 hours with a median of 6.5 hours for basic and 1 hour for inservice training (Hails and Borum, 2003). According to Maloney, Ward and Jackson (2003), police officers in the Los Angeles area do not receive adequate training in this area. Indeed, many law enforcement agencies believe that not enough time is allocated to the issue of mental health training (Barringer, Washington, 2003). McAfee and Musso (1995) have analyzed police training programs and indicated that 29 states had some type of training in dealing with mentally ill, mentally disturbed or emotionally disturbed individuals. The average amount of time devoted to issues related to all types of disabilities is 13.83 hours; the range is from two to fifty-five hours. In Illinois, the basic police patrol curriculum has included since its inception in 1980 a four-hour block of instruction entitled "Dealing with Variant Behavior" (Law Enforcement, 2001). Most Police Officers' Standards and Training Commissions (POSTs) around the nation have recognized the importance and need for law enforcement officers to have at least some training in response and interaction with persons with mental illness.

There is strong evidence to suggest that the basic training of recruits needs improvement. Basic training is very limited in the duration and depth of the curricula. The use of scenarios, role-playing and problem-based learning is minimal. Moreover, instructors have limited or no training in this area. Also, a considerable number of Field Training Officers (FTOs) also have little or no training in this area. Additionally, there is no training for dealing with stress following an encounter with a mentally ill person, despite the fact that stress training is an important aspect of policing. Police academy training covers most aspects of law enforcement and it prepares officers for physical survival but tends to ignore the psychological aspects of the profession (Kureczka, 2002).

In order to enhance the awareness training of recruits, the state's POST must review their training curricula and include mandatory training. Moreover, it is particularly important to revise the "Use of Force" training module accordingly to suit encounters with persons with mental illness. To design a basic training module that would focus on learning practical tactics through problem-based scenarios and materials would also be beneficial. Basic training methods should predominantly include simulations, role-plays, video scenarios, group discussions, reviews of policies and procedural responsibilities and analyses of case studies. Continual annual updates in curricula are also important. All Field Training Officers should have to go through special training for dealing with mental illness.

IN-SERVICE TRAINING. Annual in-service training is required by most jurisdictions. In some states a significant number of officers is attending one or another type of training in this subject area. According to Vermette, Pinals and Appelbaum in 2001–2002 in Massachusetts 73.4 percent of police officers had attended postacademy mental health training (Vermette, Pinals, and Appelbaum, 2005).

In-service training is more diverse in duration and topics from department to department than recruit training. It is usually held in a block or a single event (Sartorius and Schulze, 2005). The hours are determined by the trainer based on the amount of information to be presented. This type of training has the potential to cover different topics and provides important information to officers. The time for in-depth analysis and discussion, however, tends to be limited. According to Hails and Borum the median amount of received training was 1 hour (Hails and Borum, 2003).

In some cases, mental health training is included in in-service segments such as the use of force, variant behavior, cultural diversity and special populations. Mental health training per se though is not usually integrated into in-service training (Barringer, Washington, 2003). As part of in-service curriculum development, agency managers and experienced officers should review current policies and procedures and meet with local mental health personnel in order to foster a high level of inter-agency cooperation. This would ensure that they adequately incorporate protocols that would allow mental health personnel and assigned officers to establish rational techniques of intervention. Integrating emergency mental health treatment into crime response procedures will not only reduce an officer's frustration, but would also help to minimize fatal incidents.

ROLL CALL TRAINING. Roll call training consists of short duration training at the inception of a tour of duty. It is akin to a briefing, although it may be designed to go somewhat further than quick information dissemination. Roll call training offers the opportunity to review any potential problem situations that may occur and to reinforce officers' skills in such areas as arrests, search and seizure, the operation of emergency vehicles, the use of force, human relations, investigations, new policies and statutory laws. There are some examples of such training also addressing mental health issues. In Portland, Oregon, for example, the Crisis Intervention Teams conduct a 30-minute video and presentation session for all officers every six months in order to deliver updated information with respect to mental illness. The Portland method approach is an excellent example of training that keeps all shifts of a department on the same page. However, there are disadvantages to many roll call training programs; they can be mosaic in nature and do not always adequately cover the necessary topics. Moreover, in many cases, the instructors lack the knowledge and experience in mental health issues.

Roll call training can, however, be more effective if there is a representative from a local mental health agency present. The representative can review any problems the officer may have in identifying mental illness, in accessing the mental health system, in clarifying procedures within the mental health agency and in taking suggestions on how to improve the methods of dealing with people in crisis. This approach can increase the interaction between agencies, thus improving communication.

SPECIALIZED TRAINING. Advanced training is typically oriented toward those law enforcement officers who have volunteered for special teams that focus on dealing with persons with mental illness. One of the national surveys indicated that in 1999 around 32 percent of medium to large law enforcement agencies have specialized response to calls concerning mentally ill which is less than in 1996 with 45 percent (Deane, Steadman, Borum, Veysey, and Morrissey, 1999; Hails and Borum, 2003). According to a 1999 survey of 194 U.S. cities, more than 40% have a special program for their officers on how to handle persons with mental illness (Reed and Purse, 2001).

Specialized training addressing law enforcement responses to mentally ill people in crisis is typically done in around 40-hour blocks of instruction. Most programs are based on the Memphis Crisis Intervention Team, which has gained national recognition. A recent study from the National Institute of Justice outlined that the departments using the "Memphis model" have had lower arrest rates for persons with mental illness, more rapid response times and more frequent diversion to treatment. The concept of CIT was formed in 1983. In 1987, the Memphis, Tennessee, police department took the concept and established the Crisis Intervention Training Program, which includes the recognition of intervention techniques most effective with persons with mental illness, communication with persons with mental illness, and advice on how to de-escalate problems. The program is 40 hours beyond the normal annual week of in-service training required for all police officers. As a follow-up, the participants receive a further eight hours of interaction exposure.

This program involves law enforcement and community mental health agencies working together in partnership in developing the curriculum and providing instructors. The main focus is on the attitudes of officers. The curriculum includes fundamentals in identifying mental illness, instruction on psychotropic medications, visits to mental hospitals, training in crisis de-escalation skills, patients' rights, civil commitment law and in defense weapons. The officer is trained to resolve a mental crisis situation at the scene by using de-escalation, negotiation or verbal crisis intervention. Officers volunteer for the team and are committed to divert people with mental health problems away from the criminal justice system. Similar training approaches were repeated by law enforcement agencies in more than eighteen jurisdictions including Albuquerque, New Mexico; Portland, Ohio, Oregon; San Jose, California; Seattle, Washington and Waterloo, Iowa. Some of these newer programs improved on the initial model. In Portland, the program was enriched with such components as childhood mental disorders, cultural competency courses on how various cultural aspects might affect mental illness and a minimum of six hours role-playing. In Seattle, instructors use a virtual reality program that stimulates the symptoms of schizophrenia, and in San Diego, the standard program includes advanced training in communication skills.

In 1983, around the same time as the beginning of the program in Memphis, the city of New Orleans, Louisiana, Police Department and area mental health services established a mobile crisis service. Its main focus was to have trained volunteers responding to psychiatric emergencies, providing crisis intervention and mental health assessment.

The average volunteer was aged 30–40 and held a master's degree. All volunteers received just under three months of classroom instruction in police procedures, report writing, interaction with mentally ill individuals, basic first aid, CPR, nonviolent physical crisis intervention and safe driving techniques. In addition to the classroom instruction, all volunteers must participate in a ride-along field-training program for seven shifts (Wellborn, 1999). There are other models which differ from the Memphis CIT approach:

- Toronto has launched a 60-hour crisis-resolution safety training for offices that focuses on the principle of "isolate and contain" (Paquette, 2000).
- In Monterey County, California, an integrated, countywide training program has been established. An overseeing committee, chaired by the chief's association designee, was created and included mental health representatives. The active support of the Monterey County Mental Health Department was a key factor. The committee created a 40-hour training program that included role-playing, the interactive participation of persons with mental illness (the consumers), the identification of various symptoms and types of medication used by the consumers, crisis negotiation tactics, panel discussions, visits to interim-type housing facilities, suicide and crisis intervention training, and a review of all countrywide protocols and incident response procedures (Klein, 2002).
- Since 1995, Baltimore County, Maryland, has held a week-long training initiative to teach law enforcement officers the strategies and skills they need to respond effectively to issues related to persons with mental illness.
- In 1996, the San Diego Police Department launched the Psychiatric Emergency Response Team (PERT), which is composed of a sworn, uniformed, specially trained patrol officer and a civilian mental health clinician who respond jointly to incidents of mental health crisis.
- Another approach is the community-based disaster support, which is training in disaster intervention offered to mental health professionals in St. Louis, Missouri. The purpose is to maximize the mental health resources within communities by equipping

community leaders so that they can provide initial crisis intervention and emotional support after major disasters, when professional resources are often limited. The training team included psychologists, psychiatry residents, psychiatric nurses and specialist nurses, clinical social workers, marital and family counselors, occupational therapists, and doctoral candidates in psychology and social work. Most were recruited from university medical centers or were advanced doctoral students in social work or clinical psychology, (North and Hong, 2000).

- In 1993, the Texas legislature set a goal to have at least one specially trained officer for mental health assignments in each police jurisdiction. Each recruited officer had to go through the "Mental Health Peace Officer" course (Graffious, 1999).

In all the above programs, officers are selected based on their interest, positive attitudes, skills in communications, experience in tactics and problem solving approaches. The programs require special screening in the form of focused interviews and psychological testing. In some cases officers receive financial incentives for the specialized training.

Specialized training usually includes the following modules: recognizing mental illness, violence and mental health, psychiatric medication and the impact of such medication, substance abuse, mental health-related laws and individual rights, intervention techniques and community and family resources. Training also includes instruction in the characteristics of individual psychiatric disorders, aggressive behavior, crisis intervention and suicide, case management, special populations (e.g., the homeless, elderly, developmentally disabled, or brain damaged), officer safety, hostage negotiations and tactical considerations. Much of the training involves recognizing mental illnesses and personality disorders, in addition to applying appropriate techniques for crisis intervention. The training also addresses officer awareness, safety and tactics. Practical exercises include role-playing scenarios on individuals in crisis. During these simulations, officers demonstrate their knowledge and crisis intervention skills. Trainers then assess these skills and offer recommendations (Munetz et al., 2006).

UNIVERSITY-BASED TRAINING FOR POLICE. Higher education generally will provide police officers with better understanding of mental illness and enhanced probability for them to recognize psychiatric disorders (LaGrange, 2003). Several universities and colleges provide training for law enforcement personnel through a variety of programs. The training provided by university faculty and staff includes recognizing signs of mental illness, interacting with the mentally disturbed, the types of treatment and medication available and the possible complications of substance abuse. John Jay College in New York, for example, provides a 40-hour course on mental illness, medications and instruction on how to deal with an individual in crisis, using extensive role-playing and scenarios. Since 1998, the University of South Florida through the Division of Education and Training at the Louis de la Parte Florida Mental Health Institute has developed the CAF model for First Response for use in law enforcement training. The purpose is to teach the necessary skills and knowledge in order to help officers respond to members of the community who are suffering from symptoms of mental illness and who are in crisis. The training introduces the CAF Model for First Response, the concepts and techniques for facilitating first response situations to appropriate resolutions. The training also emphasizes the positive aspects of providing law enforcement officers with additional techniques that can be used during first response crisis situations. In addition to the above-mentioned training module, the Institute is conducting CAF "Train the Trainer" workshops to help law enforcement agencies develop a curriculum to meet the training needs of their departments. The workshops focus on providing law enforcement trainers with information on the CAF Model, training resources and strategies for the development of the curriculum. The Institute has also provided consultation for the Federal Bureau of Investigation as well as many law enforcement jurisdictions in the Tampa Bay area.

Unlike specialized training, university-based training is not so community oriented and rarely includes instruction from the families of mentally ill people, from community advocates or from consumers.

SYNOPSIS OF CURRENT TRAINING. An analysis of the above-mentioned training demonstrates that currently there are two approaches in mental health training for law enforcement personnel: (1) law enforcement based, which is predominantly awareness training (recruit training, roll call, in-service training), and (2) mental health-based specialized, which is predominantly intervention training (CIT special training, university-based training). Mental health awareness training effectively prepares recruits and officers to confront sensitive issues and to interact rationally with consumers and fellow officers. Officers should be able to recognize the importance of their role as caring social servants of the community, not just as crime fighters. The ultimate goals of awareness training are to eradicate prejudice, promote safety for officers and mentally ill individuals and to establish good relationships with consumers, which in turn should lead to a better police image and community links. Training should help to overcome some officer's prejudices concerning informational credibility of persons with mental illness. It is important not to allow police to lose valuable information (Watson, Corrigan, Ottari, 2004; Compton et al., August, 2006).

Training in mental health intervention focuses on a specialized response to "mental disturbance" and a problem-solving approach. The profound goal of intervention training is to divert consumers away from the criminal justice system and provide elements of treatment before, or even instead of, admittance to a mental health institution.

However, current limited review of the amount of training demonstrates that the consolidated training time is below 16 hours recommended by Police Executive Research Forum in 1997 as a desirable benchmark (Consensus, 1997).

Improving Law Enforcement Agency Models for Mental Health Training

To be more effective, training in awareness and intervention with respect to mental health crisis ought to be based on interagency and community shared values. It is vital that these values form the basis for law enforcement and mental health professionals so that they meet their ethical standards as professionals. These values are:

- Respecting the human rights of individuals with mental illness, their families, communities, cultures and ethnic groups.
- Approaching mental health crisis as an illness rather than a crime.
- Discouraging the promotion of prejudiced attitudes.
- Diverting mentally ill individuals away from the criminal justice system.

- Utilizing scientific approaches to mental health problems.
- Integrating different perspectives (criminal justice, mental health, communities, families, advocacy and consumers) on mental health in the quest for policies and protocols.
- Pursuing reintegration of persons with mental illness into the community and the family.

Law enforcement and mental health agencies must develop their core values on the basis of shared philosophy, which should develop from a natural extension of community policing. The philosophy statement should be in the form of a message from the police hierarchy.

Potential Challenges

The initial recruitment of police officers for specialized and intervention training could be difficult because of negative experiences and the resulting biased attitudes of a significant number of officers. Recruitment for intervention training has to be on a volunteer basis with certain screening procedures. In small law enforcement agencies this could be a problem because of limited resources. To include representatives of the community, consumers, families, advocacy, and mental health professionals into the recruitment and selection committee would be beneficial. As a long-term approach, the establishment of minimal standards for recruitment such as college education, experience in community policing, use of force "clean" record, etc., would also be productive.

The selection of officers for training must focus on individuals with some psychological, medical or paramedical knowledge in order to deal with complex, clinical material. Psychological theories, concepts and jargon can be abstract and confusing. In addition, some law enforcement officers have the perception that some criminals use mental health symptoms as an "excuse" to avoid social responsibilities and punishment.

Developing a Training Committee or Task Force

Any effectively balanced training for law enforcement officers dealing with mental health crises must be delivered through the combined efforts of several agencies. The failure of these agencies to make this connection effectively endangers the lives of citizens and law enforcement personnel. On the local and state level, successful cooperation often depends on the leadership of these agencies.

The chief executive of the law enforcement agency must initiate the formation of the task force or training committee. The committee should have a diverse membership and thus include representatives of the agency, professionals from local and state mental health services, as well as representatives from the community, and individuals with mental illness and their family members. The inclusion of representatives from the community could also enhance community relations and promote training issues on local concerns. The first step in this partnership approach might involve contact and discussion between law enforcement and selected mental health leaders. Such informal discussions could identify mutual problems, concerns and ideas. A next step in this process could involve the establishment of a liaison position in the law enforcement agency, which in turn would facilitate day-to-day communication between the law enforcement agency and various local and state services. This communication could lead to the establishment of a collaborative training committee and other mutual endeavors.

A partnership may develop in which the representatives put together a package of documents describing the nature and scope of their joint efforts. This training partnership might include the following elements:

- The defined audience of training.
- The purpose of the training agreement.
- The training objectives.
- The determination of the responsibilities of each participation agency.
- The time lines for the training implementation.
- Evaluation criteria for future program development.

The training objectives should be based on improving knowledge and skills, as well as developing specific abilities. Existing training courses and materials should help the law enforcement agency specify its training goals and objectives.

Ultimately, the focus of the training programs is on improving skills in dealing with this population and reducing violent outcomes. The objectives of such programs are as follows:

- To enhance awareness and basic understanding of mental illness, and to foster skills to help law enforcement officers in their responses to and management of individuals with mental disorders or mental illness.
- To ensure that law enforcement officers deal with mentally ill people in an appropriate manner, and that they respect the rights of these individuals.
- To minimize the risk of injury or harm to persons with mental illness, the community and the law enforcement personnel.
- To increase safety for law enforcement personnel. (Most are not trained to deal with persons with mental illness.)
- To enhance safety for mental health providers. (Most are not trained to deal with hostile situations requiring police intervention.)
- To increase safety for the public and for the family members of persons with mental illness.
- To increase safety for the inmates in jails and detention centers.
- To educate family members of persons with mental illness as primary care providers and as the first responders during mental health crisis.

Training enables officers to understand that mental illness is not a crime but a disease requiring special care. The advantage of training a police officer in this area lies in the fact that a mentally ill person is more likely to get treatment than to be arrested. Multidiscipline training approaches contains the following elements:

- Mental health institutions provide training that includes recognizing the symptoms of mental illness or emotional disturbance
- Approaches are identified for interacting with a person experiencing those symptoms
- Types of treatment and medication are identified, as well as substance abuse issues
- Law enforcement agencies must also provide close links between the criminal justice system, the health service system, and the

public as the most important component of the training strategies

This multidiscipline training approach promotes education, training, sensitivity and special care in a section of the community. Training should be cognizant of local, state and federal standards. The basic elements of the development and implementation of the training curricula should include the following:

1. Competence in communication skills.
2. Evaluation and assessment of mentally ill techniques.
3. Intervention skills and tools.
4. Community and family engagement in crisis intervention techniques.
5. Problem-solving skills.
6. Teamwork tools and approaches.
7. Community, family and interagency monitoring of mentally ill individuals.

There are numerous topics to be addressed within a complete training regimen for law enforcement personnel. A partial list of questions and topics includes the following:

Understanding mental illness

What is mental illness? What are specific mental illnesses?

Who and where are people with mental illness?

What are the differences between mental illness and developmental disabilities?

What are the differences between mental illness and neurological disorders such as epilepsy, Alzheimer's disease, Tourette's syndrome and autism?

What are the common medication and side effects?

What are co-occurring disorders?

What are the attitudes about mental illness, misconceptions, discrimination and stigma?

What are the cultural and gender differences?

Statutory influences on police responses

Federal laws.

Rehabilitation Act of 1973.

Americans with Disabilities Act of 1990.
Civil rights Act of 1983.
Local and state statutes, civil liability of police officers.
Confidentiality issues, confidentiality of medical information, police report writing, and limits of information sharing.

Police response to calls for service

On-scene assessment.
Recognizing characteristics of impairment and crisis behavior.
The signs and symptoms of mental illness-verbal and behavioral cues, medical or situational causes of crisis behavior.
Crisis intervention, de-escalation techniques and communication skills, suicide prevention and other high-risk situations.
Victim/witness assistance.

Response options

Noncustodial police options; counseling, release, and referral; voluntary emergency evaluation and noncustodial transport.
Partnerships with mental health representatives; working with community-based resources; local hospital-based psychiatric and substance abuse services; NAMI, and other advocacy organizations.
Mobile crisis teams and community-based services and supports.

Booking

Custodial police options, arresting and interviewing a suspect with mental illness.
Involuntary emergency evaluation and custodial transport.
Involuntary commitment orders and civil criteria.
Police lockup, suicide screening and medication management.

Training Cooperation

An essential aspect of improved police training is the expansion of the working relationship between law enforcement and local mental health service providers. In Illinois, a survey revealed that 74 percent of the responding law enforcement agencies had no local agreements with local mental health providers (Law Enforcement, 2001). In addition, the Illinois task force survey revealed that 83 percent of the responding law enforcement agency had no written operational policies in the area of dealing with mentally ill individuals.

The agreement should be flexible, capable of being amended to suit changing conditions, and should serve as a focal point for combined ventures designed to foster closer working relationships between law enforcement and mental health service providers.

Training Development: The Illinois Model

In 2003, law enforcement and mental health leaders from Illinois held a three-day summit addressing mutual concerns. The Illinois Summit of Law Enforcement and Mental Health Providers identified four levels of training for development:

Level 1: *The development and implementation of "Train-the-Trainer Summits" for certified trainers and appropriate mental health staff who will conduct the police-mental health section of the basic training course for police and correctional academies statewide.* The "Train-the-Trainer Summits" should also help law enforcement agencies develop a training curriculum to meet the needs of their departments. These Summits should focus on providing the law enforcement instructor with information on the training resources and strategies for developing the curriculum. The focus should be on developing effective training courses and methodology. The course will include a trainer's manual, which contains full instructions and a variety of role-play scenarios for training the police on mental health issues; an officer's guide, who summarizes the basic information and tools on how to deal with mentally ill people; and videotapes to help the instructor use the trainer's manual. Trainers who have knowledge and experience in both mental health and juvenile justice must be included.

Level 2: *The development and implementation of "Train-the-Supervisor Summits" for police chiefs and sheriffs.* An executive management program should be designed to facilitate coordination among police chiefs, sheriffs, state and county mental health officials, providers, family advocates (NAMI), and consumer/survivors of mental illness. The training must also provide skills, tools and tactics for law enforcement executives to de-escalate situations involving persons with mental illness or developmental disability problems. Executives should receive information about the various mental illnesses, developmental disabilities, crisis intervention techniques, community resources and any other major areas that would be useful for them in helping people in crisis. This training should produce confident supervisors who respond professionally in an empathetic and calming manner.

Level 3: *Improved and expanded recruit (pre-service/academy) training.* This training module should be increased from four to eight hours. The module should focus on techniques for the identification of mental illness, drug and alcohol abuse and responses to related violent behavior. Training Field Training Officers in mental health awareness is important, so that they can correctly evaluate the new recruits. Field training programs can be an effective managerial tool through which law enforcement administrators can manage the transition to nonviolent encounters with mentally ill people in the community.

Level 4: *Provide in-service training via roll call training.* Roll call training provides the opportunity for reviewing problem situations that may have arisen, or for initiating discussions on relevant topics. A mental health representative could be invited to review potential problems for officers dealing with the mental health system, and to clarify procedures within the mental health system. This type of program increases interaction and improves links between agencies.

Instruction through agency in-service training units could be conducted in four eight-hour blocks or in a single session with the hours determined by the trainer, based on the amount of information presented. In-service training could be aimed at call takers, dispatchers, front desk personnel, new recruits, patrol officers and deputy sheriffs, as well as some detectives and drug-enforcement officers.

Illinois officials identified financial resources as a major concern. To minimize training costs, law enforcement agencies should use informal cross-training opportunities in the community. Organizing frequent training visits to mental health institutions for law enforcement personnel is not costly, except in terms of staff time, and yet it allows officers to get information and make useful direct contacts. Some police departments currently use incentives as a means of attracting officers to participate in training and in the mental health response team (Bower and Pettit, 2001).

Summit leaders also noted that regions and communities throughout the nation have numerous resources for addressing these training challenges. Some may include the following:

Local colleges and universities
Community mental health centers
Local advocacy groups such as NAMI

Mental health associations
Sample cooperative agreements
Policy documents
Videotape training references
Training modules
General documents (Issues and Approaches, Hoover, 2002)

The Illinois Summit leaders stated that there are numerous training audiences within every law enforcement agency: law enforcement executives and supervisors, police and corrections officers, 911 operators, trainers and instructors. In order to provide effective training for a law enforcement agency, departments need to:

- Obtain information regarding the position of each participant within the law enforcement agency.
- Determine the educational and cultural background of the audience.
- Identify their existing knowledge of encounters with mentally ill people.
- Identify the type of knowledge or skills the audience needs to gain from the training project.
- Understand the attitudes of the participants towards the training in mental health crisis.

Training will not be effective unless the perspective of the audience is understood first. Members of the audience are likely to respond according to their educational and cultural backgrounds, professional and personal profiles, knowledge of mental health problems and their positions within the agency. Thus, training objectives and approaches may vary with different audiences.

Conclusion

There are many successful training programs around the country that have demonstrated the effectiveness of newly introduced knowledge and skills to law enforcement officers. According to Vickers (2000), in Memphis, before they set up their own Crisis Intervention Team (CIT) model, officers spent four to six hours at the medical center waiting for the person to be admitted to a hospital. This waiting time is now down to about 15 minutes. Additional benefits of that training program include reduced stigma and perception of the danger attached to mental illness, increased involvement of officers on calls related to mental illness, reduced use of deadly force, reduced use of restraints, fewer injuries to officers and citizens, greater flexibility in the use of misdemeanor charges, lower arrest rates, a 2.5–3 percent decline in the number of consumers sent to jail, relief to an overburdened criminal justice system, initial reports written by officers enabling far better preparation for doctors and nurses, officers spending less time in ER and finally, and a decrease by almost 40 percent in the number of injuries suffered by individuals with mental illnesses during the course of their encounter with the police.

Between 1993–1999, the Seattle PD hostage-negotiation team was called an average of 38 times a year to respond to people in mental health crises. After the crisis intervention program was launched, the call-outs dropped to eighteen, and suicide intervention call-outs have dropped 60 percent (Fryer, 2001). In the San Diego Police Department, the Psychiatric Emergency Response Team (PERT) (comprised of law enforcement and mental health personnel) in its first year achieved significant reductions in the time required for police intervention, as well as a reduced arrest rate of persons with mental illness (Margolis, 2002). In 1999, the Albuquerque Police Department, which also trained personnel according to a CIT model, reported that officers arrested, transported to jail, or otherwise took into protective custody fewer than ten percent of those people with mental illnesses with whom they came into contact. The fall in use of SWAT was reported at 58 percent (Bower and Pettit, 2001).

The effectiveness of the new programs has been measured in overall impact and also in the savings of resources. For example, a study of three police departments that had implemented innovative solutions (Memphis, Knoxville, and Birmingham) demonstrated that 34.7 percent were resolved at the scene; subjects were referred to long-term mental health specialists in thirteen percent of cases, and 45.7 percent were immediately transported to a treatment facility or were admitted to hospital. Only 6.7 percent of the incidents from the total survey resulted in arrests (Borum et al., 1998).

Dealing with mental health crises in local communities has increasingly affected law enforcement agencies nationwide. To expect one agency to provide the solution for this critical social problem is unrealistic. Only through proper training and interagency cooperation can a viable solution be found. Permanent and continuous training approaches should serve as an "icebreaker" to the traditionally isolated and separate training sessions of independent agencies. This approach will create new and promising ways for dealing with mentally ill individuals.

Progress in improved mental health and law enforcement services requires action on many fronts: improved basic training, greater attention to mental illness within the in-service training system, better coordination between mental health and law enforcement agencies and improved risk assessment and management strategies within the criminal justice system.

Community agencies, families, consumers, as well as officers, have all been an integral part of this movement to provide officers with additional tools with which to address the concerns of mentally ill persons. Maintaining the safety of both officers and members of the community is the central focus of this combined effort.

REFERENCES

Autopsy: Cops shot man many times. (2007, March 3). *Chicago Tribune,* p.7.

Bailey, A., Barr, O., & Bunting, B. (2001, August). Police attitudes toward people with intellectual disability: An evaluation of awareness training. *Journal of Intellectual Disability Research, 45*(4), 344–350.

Barringer, T., & Washington, P. (2003, July). Utilization of a systems training model to enhance community policing with seriously mentally ill persons. *Law Enforcement Executive Forum, 3*(3), 1–16.

Boles, A., Wolfe, D., & Fulton, F. (2001). *Police/mental health cooperative response to individuals with developmental disabilities: Evaluation and recommendations.* Muir Beach, CA: Critical Focus, Inc.

Borum, R. (2000). Improving high risk encounters between people with mental illness and the police. *Journal of the American Academy of Psychiatry and the Law, 28,* 332–337.

Borum, R., Deane, M., Steadman, H. J., & Morrissey, J. (1998). Police perspectives on responding to mentally ill people in crisis: Perceptions of program effectiveness. *Behavioral Sciences and the Law, 16,* 393–405.

Bower, D., & Pettit, G. (2001). The Albuquerque Police Department's Crisis Intervention Team: A report card. *FBI Law Enforcement Bulletin, 70*(2), 1–6.

Community Governance & Intergovernmental Partnerships. (2000). Community policing and the mentally ill: The community mental health officer. Available online at www.communitypolicing.org/publications/exchange/e32_00e32

Compton, M.T., Esterberg, M. L., McGee, R., Kotwicki, R. J., & Oliva, J. R. (2006, August). Brief reports: Crisis intervention team training: Changes in knowledge, attitudes, and stigma related to schizophrenia. *Psychiatric Services, 57,* 1199–1202.

Council of State Governments. (2002, June). *Criminal justice/mental health consensus project report.* New York: Author.

Criminal Justice/Mental Health Consensus Project fact sheet. (2002). Available online at www.consensusproject.org/general/about-problem

Deane, M., Steadman, H., Borum, R., Veysey B., & Morrissey, J. (1999). Emerging partnerships between mental health and law enforcement. *Psychiatric Services, 50,* 99–101.

Fry, A., O'Riordan, D., & Geanellos, R. (2002, July). Social control agents or front-line careers for people with mental health problems: Police and mental health services in Sydney, Australia. *Health & Social Care in Community, 10*(4), 277–286.

Fryer, A. (2001, September). Police learn about mentally ill. *Seattle Times.* Available online at http://seattletimes.nwsource.com/html/local news/13433 6641_mental103m.html

Graffious, D. (1999). Mental health peace officer. Available online at www.utexas.edu/cee/dec/tcleose/assets/mental/pdf

Hails, J., & Borum, R. (2003). Police training and specialized approaches to respond to people with mental illnesses. *Crime and Delinquency, 49*(1), 52–61.

Hoover, L. T. (2002, November). Presentation. *Dealing with persons with mental illness: An overview of issues.* Bloomington, IL: Illinois Law Enforcement Training and Standards Board.

Illinois Law Enforcement Training and Standards Board. (2001, March). *Law enforcement and mental health interaction in responding to persons with mental illness.* Task force report. Springfield, IL: Author.

Jamieson, R. L., & Wilson, K. C. (2000, May 25). Mental illness frequently deepens tragedy of policy shootings. Northwest. Available online at http://seatlepi.nwsource.com/local/shot252.shtml

Keram, E. A. (2005, March). Commentary: A multidisciplinary approach to developing mental health training for law enforcement. *Journal of the American Academy of Psychiatry and the Law Online, 33*(1), 47–49.

Klein, M. (2002). Law enforcement's response to people with mental illness. *FBI Law Enforcement Bulletin, 71*(2), 11–14.

Kureczka, A. (2002). Surviving assaults: After the physical battle ends, the psychological battle begins. *FBI Law Enforcement Bulletin, 71*(2), 11–14.

LaGrange, T. (2003, Spring). The role of police education in handling cases of mental disorder. *Criminal Justice Review, 28,* 88–112.

Lamb, R., Weinberger, L., & DeCuir, W. (2002, October). The police and mental health. *Psychiatric Services, 53*(10), 1266–1271.

Los Angeles Police Department. (2002). Consent decree mental illness project recommendations. Available online at www.lapdonline.org/pdf_files/boi/consent_decree_mental_ill_supp_rpt.pdf

Maloney, M. P., Ward, M., & Jackson, C. M. (2003). Study reveals that more mentally ill offenders are entering jail. *Corrections Today, 65*(2), 100–106.

Margolis, G. (2002). *Criminal justice system and the mentally ill. FDCH congressional testimony.* Available online at http://web14.epnet.com/citation.asp?tb

McAfee, J. K., & Musso, S. L. (1995, January). Training police officers about persons with disabilities. *Remedial & Special Education, 16*(1), 53–63.

Munetz, M. R., Morrison, A., Krake, J., Young, B., & Woody, M. (2006, November). State mental health policy: Statewide implementation of the crisis intervention team program: The Ohio model. *Psychiatric Services, 57,* 1569–1571.

Murphy, G. R. (1986). *Improving the police response to the mentally disabled.* Washington, DC: Police Executive Research Forum.

Norris, C., & Cooke, E. (2000, July). Mental health training scheme for police officers. *Professional Nurse, 15*(10), 655–658.

North, C., & Hong, B. (2000). Project CREST: A new model for mental health intervention after a community disaster. *American Journal of Public Health, 90*(7), 1057–1058.

Paquette, M. (2000). Editorial. *Perspectives in Psychiatric Care, 3*(2), 39–20.

Price, M., & Pinals, D. A. (2006). Law enforcement and mental health professionals: A collaborative approach to training. *Law Enforcement Executive Forum, 6*(3), 61–73.

Price, M. (2005, March). Commentary: The challenge of training police officers. *Journal of the American Academy of Psychiatry the Law Online, 33,* 50–54.

Read, K., & Purse, M. (2001). Police handling of the mentally ill. Available online at http://bipolar.about.co/library/weekly/aa010212a.htm

Roberts, R. C. (1976). Police social workers: A history. *Social Work, 21*(4), 294–298.

Sartorius, N., & Schulze, H. (2005). Reducing the stigma of mental illness: A report from a global programme of the World Psychiatric Association. Cambridge University Press.

Teese, C., & Wormer, J. (1975, Summer). Mental health training and consultation with suburban police. *Community Mental Health Journal, 11*(2), 115–121.

Teller, J. L. S., Munetz, M. R., Gil, K. M., & Ritter, C. (2006, February 1). Crisis intervention team training for police officers responding to mental disturbance calls. *Psychiatric Services, 57*(2), 232–237.

Vermette, H. S., Pinals, D. A., & Appelbaum, P. S. (2005). Mental health training for law enforcement professionals. *Journal of the American Academy of Psychiatry the Law Online, 33*(1), 42–46.

Vickers, B. (2000). Memphis, Tennessee, Police Department's Crisis Intervention Team. Bulletin from the field, practitioner perspectives. Washington, DC: Bureau of Justice Assistance. Available online at www.ncjrs.org/txtfiles1/bja/182501.txt

Walsh, J., & Witte, P. (1975, Fall). Police training in domestic crises. A suburban approach. *Community Mental Health Journal, 11*(3), 301–306.

Watson, A., Corrigan, P., & Ottari, V. (2004, January). Police officers' attitudes toward and decisions about persons with mental illness. *Psychiatric Services, 55*(1), 49–53.

Wells, W., & Schafer, J. A. (2006). Officer perceptions of police responses to persons with a mental illness. *Policing: An International Journal of Police Strategies &*

Management, 29(4), 578–601.

Wellborn, J. (1999). Responding to individuals with mental illness. *FBI Law Enforcement Bulletin, 68*(11), 6–10.

Chapter 8

COLLABORATIVE AGREEMENTS WITH MENTAL HEALTH AGENCIES

THOMAS J. JURKANIN
VLADIMIR A. SERGEVNIN

At some point, law enforcement professionals and mental health care providers are bound to come into contact with the same persons with mental illness. However, professionals in both segments of social service often experience frustration at the limitations of their institutional potential. Law enforcement or mental health alone cannot implement and advance multidimensional services to individuals in mental health crisis. Society is so complex today that individual agencies cannot deal with new challenges and problems without interdependent collaboration. A majority of departments with specialized response program and collaborative agreements rated themselves more effective in dealing with mentally ill persons in crisis. Law enforcement benefits when collaborative partnerships are established to implement interagency service models, which increase the amount of shared information and best practices, eliminate duplication of services; improve consumer's lives and enhance law enforcement community image (Deane, Steadman, Borum, Veysey, and Morrissey, January 1999; In Place of Fear, 2006). The chapter is designed to help law enforcement departments and their partners better understand, develop, and improve effective collaborative agreements. Specifically, this chapter addresses new opportunities and possible solutions for establishing this collaboration. We cannot address every factor that may shape collaboration between officers and mental health providers. Each state and county is different and requires stakeholders to prioritize their performance of tasks. What this chapter offers law enforcement officers are basic guidelines to observe when establishing collaborative agreements. The ideological background of the chapter is a reminder that every individual with mental health problems deserves to be treated with courtesy, respect, and fairness. When mental health providers and law enforcement officers work together and help each other, the effectiveness of the entire social structure increases.

Need for Collaboration

It has long been recognized that law enforcement collaborative agreements with mental health agencies is the key approach in dealing with the national mental health service crisis (Finn and Sullivan,1987; Siegel, 1990; White and Harris, 2001; Landsberg, 2002; Jenkins, 2002; Joint Committee On Human Rights, 2004). However, collaborative agreements for addressing these issues have been slow to develop. Only around 30 percent of the police departments have partnership agreements (Landsberg, 2002). This is due in part to the different perspectives of mental health and law enforcement agencies, and to lack of an integrated vision and culture that addresses both the social and legal needs of mentally ill individuals. Collaborative agencies have diverse organizational cultures. Even the term "collaborative agreement" has different meanings to various agencies.

Traditionally, law enforcement personnel and mental health institutions existed in a self-isolationist environment because the historical social designs of these two professions are different.

	Law Enforcement Agencies	*Mental Health Institutions*
Mission	*Public safety, crime fighting, intervention, imposing sanctions*	*Diagnose, emergency treatment, Preventive care*
Focus	*Violator with criminal behavior*	*Patient with mental illness*
Methods	*Use of force, isolation from community*	*Medication, adoption to community adaptation*
Period of interaction	*Brief contact*	*Time-consuming care*

With the advent of the community-policing concept (discussed in detail in Chapter 9), the potential for collaborative efforts have become more promising (Jurkanin, Sergevnin, and Bender, 2003).

Collaboration is defined as a system that integrates the resources and delivery of appropriate mental health care services through processes or techniques used by different entities in order to control or influence the quality, accessibility, utilization or costs and prices or outcomes of such services provided to a defined enrollee population. The vital components of collaboration are: stakeholders interest in collaboration; a trusting relationship; a shared vision and common goals; expertise; teamwork strategies; open communication; motivated partners; means to implement and sustain the collaboration; and an action plan (Rinehart, Laszlo, and Briscoe, 2002).

Collaborative agreements between law enforcement and mental health agencies are important on many different levels. For the consumers and theirs families who may initially seek help in either system, having a provider who can provide a full range of services improves substantially the quality of treatment received. Mental health professionals are less likely to feel overwhelmed by consumers need for safety, or their need for help negotiating the criminal justice system. Law enforcement agencies are not trained to be professional mental health providers, but assumed this role for social necessity reasons. In times of decreased funding, government has to find humane and effective resolution to protect one of the most vulnerable segments of society. For all the stakeholders, it is important to create collaborative treatment models that reflect multidimensional needs of different social institutions and citizens.

Philosophical Background

Collaborative agreements represent a significant shift in collective psychology and understanding the way of dealing with consumers for law enforcement and mental health administrators, providers, families, and other stakeholders. The objective of collaborative agreements is to bring individual agencies and members of communities together in an environment of support to systematically solve existing and emerging problems that could not be solved by one stakeholder alone.

A fundamental theoretical issue of collaboration is the social contract concept. According to the theories of Hobbes, Locke, and

Rousseau a social contract is the voluntary agreement among individuals by which organized society is brought into being and invested with the right to secure mutual protection and welfare (Webster's, 1996). Social contract theory is a continuation of the tradition of perfectionism in an effort to enhance the quality of life in a free society. It requires continuous effort to establish new forms of interactions between individuals, social entities, and government for the benefit of people. The most important implication of social contract theory is that it opens the search for forms of association "that defends and protects the person and goods of each associate with all the common force" (Rousseau, 1762). For Hobbes, Locke, and Hume, the fundamental idea of social contract is that individuals establish laws and institutions. For Rousseau, the idea of social contract requires continuous contracting (Affeldt, 2000). The individual has to continuously search for new forms of common life on the basis of contracting with others. The approach of contracting is more flexible and allows free choice in the forms of collaboration. The most important lesson from social contract theory is that it acknowledges the role of people in constructing social relationships in new forms continuously.

Social contract theory in the history of Anglo-American philosophy is predominantly viewed as the foundation of an abstract model of an ideal society. Modern American society developed certain traits that promote the adoption of collaborative agreements between different social entities:

SELF-GOVERNING. Centralization becomes inevitable when traditionally fragmented governments are faced with problems that exceed their boundaries, such as dealing with persons who are mentally ill. However, centralized response often cannot be fulfilled through political collaboration at federal and state levels because the constitutions of these entities are based on division of authority, or stated differently–fragmentation. The only channel for centralization is local collaboration among agencies with similar goals. Local governmental agencies and public associations are taking on more responsibility for solutions to issues that have traditionally been state jurisdiction. The self-governing tendency becomes especially important in times of financial crisis when states have very limited recourses and are forced to abandon various social programs.

QUALITY OF COMMUNITY. Quality of community issues, particularly unemployment, crime, mental health and homelessness of citizens and families, are emerging as key areas of public concern.

PRIVATIZATION. State agencies are examining the effectiveness of addressing common issues and services which potentially can reduce duplication of cost and effort. Local governments favor social contracts and collaborative agreements because they redirect the responsibilities and reduce expenditures. Law enforcement and mental health agencies understand the need to formally address not only their roles in the criminal justice and health segments of society, but also their social roles in their community.

A serious challenge arising from this approach is whether resources exist for transition from "formal public sector" to "informal sector" of collaboration and networking. It is useful to make conceptual distinctions between informal collaborative agreements and formal service-giving institutions. The transition from institutional services to collaborative agreements is not necessarily without difficulty. Another important challenge of collaboration is that collaboration is the process but not the final point of partnering, sharing, and communicating to achieve common goals. The nature of collaboration is dynamic and requires continuous efforts to improve the interdependency.

The Scope of Collaborative Agreements

There is a wide range of collaborative or partnership arrangements which criminal justice and mental health agencies enter into with other institutions or organizations. Although the current scope of collaboration agreements is a recent development, partnership endeavors involving the criminal justice and mental health sectors have been documented since the 1960s (Gerdes et al., 2001).

TRAINING-BASED STAGE. The first attempts to establish interagency response to individuals in mental crisis focused on collaboration in training provided to law enforcement officers (Consent decree, 2002). Various training programs were developed in order to overcome law enforcement officers' prejudices toward consumers. Although the impact of this approach was positive, criminal justice and mental health systems were still dissatisfied with the quality of service and the level of specialized response.

AGENCY-BASED STAGE. From the 1970s the main approach shifted to collaborative agreements in establishing specialized responders to calls involved mental health issues. The ideology, principles, and goals of collaboration led to the development of several models that have implications for integration of mental health providers. Specialized responder models have identified established programs that are effective in addressing the needs of mentally ill:

- *Mental health-based mental health responders model* with a cooperative agreement allowing mobile mental health crisis team to provide assistance to police;
- *Law enforcement-based specialized law enforcement responders* with a collaboration agreement between law enforcement and mental health entities to provide specialized training to selected police officers who formed Crisis Intervention Teams (CIT). The Memphis Police Department is credited with pioneering this approach;
- *Law enforcement-based mental health responders* with a collaborative agreement for a civilian mental health specialist in charge of providing on-site assistance through a Community Service Officer program (CSO), pioneered by the Birmingham Police Department (Consent Decree, 2002).

One study comparing all three models found that lower rates of arrests, better response time and heightened law enforcement satisfaction was found for the police-based responders approach vs. mental health-based responses (Deane et al., 1999). The programs have notable differences, partly due to the resources, program structure, and staff expertise of their respective approaches. Each, however, requires some level of collaboration between law enforcement and mental health professionals. Generally, these strategies decrease the arrest rates from 21 percent for contacts between nonspecialized police officers and persons who were apparently ill to less than 7 percent (Lamb, Weiberger and Decuir, 2002). Across Los Angeles, Memphis, and Birmingham, only 6.7 percent of the "mental disturbance" calls resulted in arrest (Arons, 2000).

Early evidence of these collaborative models demonstrates positive impact of establishing collaborative entities like Crisis Intervention Teams (Margolis, 2002,). The success of the models was mirrored in the criminal justice mental health standards adopted by the American Bar Association (1984), to include: (1) provide specialized training to assist officers; (2) use qualified professionals to provide such training; (3) create written policies and procedures for crisis encounters (Reid and Silver, 2002); and (4) collaborate with mental health agencies on developing policies and procedures.

However, it became clear that there are definite limitations of the agency-based model agreements:

- The agency's culture and policies dominate each of the models.
- The approach ignores consumers and communities.
- Partners are not equal in the influence, the quality, the accessibility, and utilization of costs.
- Organizations may not have a common goal.
- There are few established partnerships with federal, state and private agencies in reducing barriers to services and increasing resources and funding.

When local agencies attempt to overcome organizational boundaries for collaboration they are under the pressure of often contradictory motivations such as "offender punishment," "keeping society safe" and "treatment and care" (Lavender, 2002). Agencies and organizations involved in collaboration are following their own motivations for using agreements, but they are surprisingly similar: (a) to ensure a cost-effective service system; (b) efficient utilization of resources; (c) to improve access to mental health care; (d) to reduce their own responsibility; and (e) to ensure treatment instead of punishment. Today, local governments and agencies are launching a new stage of collaboration that potentially can reduce the gaps and pitfalls of traditional approaches.

Equal Partnership

The agency-based stage of collaboration depended individually on law enforcement, or mental health, or advocacy groups' initiative, rather than equal partners with a shared vision. Even recently, collaboration is viewed only as cooperation among formally constituted criminal justice and mental health systems. According to recent research, in New York City the Emergency Services Unit has no ties with community advocacy groups or consumers (Criminal Justice/ Mental Health Consensus Project, 2002). In order to attain positive outcomes, it is imperative that all the stakeholders, including consumers, families, communities, advocacy groups, social service agencies, and criminal justice and mental health entities, have to develop new models based on equal partnership and synergetic approaches. Stakeholders have many common concerns, including, most notably:

- Overlapping interests: partners are usually joined by mission, having shared service interests and obligations. From a process perspective, they are likely to share an interest in resolving the problem cost-effectively.
- Interdependence: no stakeholder can dictate an outcome by imposing a resolution on the other.

Four key factors outline the necessity of establishing equal partnership collaborative agreements. First, many advocacy groups, criminal justice and mental health agencies reported an increasing awareness of the need for services that address the problems of individuals with mental illness. Agencies and communities are struggling with limited resources and feel unprepared to respond to the complex needs of consumers. Second, training programs for law enforcement personnel are not enough for responding to this complicated social issue. Mental illness is still highly stigmatized, and prejudice is shown toward consumers and their family members. Collaborative agreements are rarely addressing this side of the problem. Third, criminal justice and mental health agencies have a tendency to minimize the importance of community, families and advocacy work, because of the institutional self-service mentality. Fourth, it is impossible in times of limited financial resources to rely only on criminal justice and mental health budgets, while ignoring community and family potential.

Collaborative agreements created among all stakeholders promote synergetic rather than an uncoordinated approach. The fundamental goals of collaborative agreements must be practical and focused, primarily to (1) decrease the amount of violent encounters between law enforcement officers and customers, and (2) divert individuals in crisis from the criminal justice to mental health system. On the county level, there are already in place many commissions, centers, and other entities for promoting interagency collaboration.

Collaboration between stakeholders and mental health providers is a relationship consisting of mutual care patterns of information and resources sharing, consultation and team communication. To meet the community and other stakeholder's expectations and make the collaboration solid it is important to identify the framework of responsibilities of each agency or stakeholder:

Criminal Justice	*Mental health*	*Community*	*Family*	*Advocacy*	*Social Services*
Rehabilitation Prevention Cross-training Crime management	Treatment Rehabilitation Prevention Cross-training Disease management	Rehabilitation Housing Income support Job training	Care Rehabilitation Housing Income support	Representation Protection Cross-training	Rehabilitation Housing Income support Job training Cross-training

Collaborative agreements have to be viewed as an attempt to restore mental health service on the basis of social support from different segments of society employing a community policing approach. The ideology of restoration appeared in the literature on the brink of the century (Joint Committee, 2000). With the advent of the community-policing concept, the potential for equal partnership collaborative efforts has become more promising.

Collaborative agreements among stakeholders promote a preventive and problem-solving approach. The following guiding principles can help to shape decisions on mental health and other stakeholder's cooperative agreement ventures:

- Consumers are the priority in collaborative agreements and will receive nondiscriminatory service from all the stakeholders.
- Collaborative agreements promote safety for consumers, service providers, community, and families.
- All stakeholders are involved in planning and delivery of service.
- One agency should not dominate in decision-making. The purpose is to enhance the level of coordination among all stakeholders.

- Agreements should provide accountability to the consumers, community, families, and stakeholders.
- Agreements should help prevent duplication of agencies' services.
- Provision of more centralized and systemic approaches is important.
- New investments and redirecting of existing resources will be required.

These principles are based on one overarching goal: enhancing communication inside the system of agencies interacting with persons with mentally illness. The framework is seeking to improve the quality of procedures and removing obstacles that hinder successful contacts with mentally ill persons.

Goals

The various groups of society represented by the collaborative partners bring different interests into the venture but common goals and vision. A statement of shared goals is the foundation of all strategy, tactics and implementation. For this purpose collaborative agreements pursue the following goals:

- Create an integrated collaborative system with the focus on mentally ill customers.
- Ensure establishment of the highest standards and services.
- Prevent physical harm to persons with mental illness and law enforcement personnel.
- Maintain the dignity of the person suffering from mental illness.
- Encourage providing long-term intervention and treatment.
- Joint treatment planning, in which all stakeholders decide which pays for what and when.
- Rationalize the usage of resources; maximize value of funds, and reduce the cost of mental health services.
- Clarify which agency is responsible for specific services, such as transportation, or community-based services.
- Ensure that information sharing confidentiality issues are implementing by all stakeholders.
- Develop joint protocols to ensure efficiency across systems.

- Break down barriers between agencies.
- Emphasize diversion from criminal justice system, recovery, and rehabilitation.
- Put in place a regional support system for local communities, families, and providers.
- Ensure productive partnership across geographical and organizational boundaries.
- Put in place regional cooperative links that supports local communities, families, and providers.
- Set benchmarks for the measurement of further progress and improved services.

Common goals and vision is the basis for trusting partnership.

Current Challenges

There are numerous obstacles that undermine collaborative efforts. These must be addressed in order to develop successful community-based collaborative agreements between all stakeholders.

LEADERSHIP. There are two sides to the leadership challenge. *First,* leaders of collaborative agencies often view the endeavor as something important, but not requiring close participation. *Second,* the coordinator of collaboration between stakeholders may not possess strong leadership skills, and is unable to get support from the agencies and communities.

MENTAL HEALTH HOSPITALS. The decision-making processes and professional paradigms in state institutions may be different from private institutions. Similar to law enforcement, there is not uniformity of thought among mental health institutions regarding the appropriate policies, procedures and protocols for addressing the needs of patients or determinations of pending crisis. Given this lack of uniformity it is possible for mental health institutions and professionals to send differing and confusing messages to law enforcement personnel. Many mental health agencies are unable to assist law enforcement, no matter how philosophical supportive they may be. The willingness and ability of local community mental health agencies to provide support and service for police may vary greatly from community to community. Many factors contribute to this, including the availability of resources to provide around the clock service and the perceptions of community mental health leaders regarding acceptable levels of risk for their personnel. Contact with a person in crisis outside of the clinical environment can pose a different set of challenges to mental health providers.

LAW ENFORCEMENT CULTURE. Officers frequently see no resolution to repeat calls and situations with the same persons. The revolving door of dealing with persons who are mentally ill is frustrating and time-consuming for responding officers. Oftentimes officers express attitudes of hopelessness related to developing effective interventions. This view often extends to their views of the community-based mental health system, which is charged with providing care and support for the repeat problems they encounter. The cynicism of officers regarding effective intervention and support will be a challenge for each department seeking improved approaches for dealing with persons in crisis.

The risk of dealing with violent consumers necessarily affects the views of law enforcement. Law enforcement officers must be constantly vigilant in assessing for violence in their interactions with citizens. Past interactions in which officers have been subjected to violent encounters increases the officers' wariness in dealing with persons in crisis. Experts indicate that on occasion understandably cautious approaches may exacerbate the behaviors of a person in crisis. Yet, prudence dictates that officers treat persons in crisis with caution and be on guard for potentially violent encounters.

Law enforcement culture supports short, not long-term, interactions. In most cases there are more incentives to "drop patients" than to follow through and identify longer-term solutions for persons who are mentally ill. In many communities the call volume for police departments does not permit intensive problem solving. Most departments seek to decrease response times to citizen calls. This works against engaging in time-consuming problem-solving practices. In general, the culture of law enforcement supports getting the immediate situation under control as opposed to developing long-term solutions to recurring behavior problems. This orientation is an obstacle to developing ongoing law enforcement mechanisms for addressing the issues of persons who are mentally ill in the community.

COMMON VISION AND IDEOLOGY. Trust and common vision of the problem and possible solutions is the crucial characteristic of collaborative agreements. Mistrust may originate in hesitation to share resources under difficult economic and financial circumstances. Open communication should reduce mistrust among all the stakeholders and help to understand the advantages of equal collaborative agreements. Nevertheless, because of institutional rules and regulations some law enforcement and mental health agencies are not willing to share information (criminal records, personal medical records, etc.).

TRANSPORTATION. The lack of transportation agreements and resources can be a major problem for local law enforcement agencies. This is particularly true for many sheriff's departments, the agencies most frequently charged with responsibility for transportation. County sheriffs are often placed in the difficult position of dedicating scarce human resources to transport persons who are mentally ill hundreds of miles to institutions out of their county. Frequently, families aren't available or won't take responsibility. The result is the sheriff is forced to reallocate deputies away from law enforcement in order to transport the patient. This can be problematic in that most deputies are not properly trained to assist the person and the situation can degenerate into deeper problems.

INFORMATION SHARING AND COMMUNICATION. Currently, only about 40 percent of local authorities have adequate systems for sharing information (Mental Health Information Strategy, March 2001). It is essential that mental health and law enforcement agencies dramatically improve the level and kinds of information to be shared at the local level. Clearly, it is important to create protocols which respect patient rights. However, it is also important to get essential information to the responding officers in a timely fashion. The lack of adequate information has and will continue to intensify dangerous situations and interactions on the street. An analysis of practices in many states reveals that the mental health and law enforcement infrastructure provides numerous obstacles to effective integration. Protective attitudes have fostered an isolationist mindset in various agencies, creating barriers to services integration. In light of current information technology, there is no physical rational for lack of information access. Lack of coordination in sharing of crisis relevant information combined with confusion over patient confidentiality serves to stymie mental health and law enforcement cooperation. Often in the absence of clear understandings or protocols the interpretation of what can be shared and not shared is left to the individual interpretation of the on-duty mental health provider. This is particularly difficult when the mental health agency does not have clear policies and procedures for dealing with requests for information. The confusion over what can and cannot be shared and the lack of consistency in providing information is a source of frustration for many law enforcement agencies.

FUNDING AND RESOURCES. Lack of funds and resources dedicated to deploying mental health professionals and properly trained law enforcement personnel is an obstacle to creating safe and effective measures to deal with persons who are mentally ill in crisis. Crisis can hit any time. In order to be effective trained personnel need to be available all of the time. This is often a greater financial and personnel burden than most community law enforcement and mental health agencies are prepared to handle. Thus, officers continue to encounter persons in crises at all hours of the night without adequate professional caregiver back-up or support. Many communities lack any significant mental health resources, particularly rural areas. This lack of mental health resources is compounded by the fact that rural police departments are smaller and lack the budgets and rarely can spare the manpower to specially train officers in techniques related to dealing with in-crisis persons. In communities where there is little training and few mental health resources, the jail may serve as the only alternative for dealing with persons in crises. This leads to greater financial problems for the sheriff and rarely effectively addresses the needs of the patient–indeed most of the time exacerbates the crisis. The separate and frequently fragmented law enforcement and mental health systems is often an obstacle to effective resource sharing. The resources for each system are designed for different ends and are rarely oriented to meet the needs of the person with mental illness at the moment he/she is in crises.

COMMUNITY AWARENESS AND PARTICIPATION. Most citizens and communities are not focused on addressing the needs of mentally ill persons. Community apathy and lack of understanding and knowledge by citizens is a major obstacle in efforts to get political and funding support for proactive initiatives. Ultimately, police training and programs for persons with mental illness must compete in the budget with other community needs and desires. The lack of effective local advocates and the ignorance of the public make it difficult to secure the necessary political support to fund initiatives for persons with mental illness. The lack of community shelters and other support systems are evidence of the apathy and lack of political support. Apathy in some neighborhoods and communities has been replaced by fear and antagonism. Numerous examples exist of neighborhoods and communities opposing support homes, clinics and other services for persons with mental illness. Rarely does this opposition translate into better programs for persons in crises. Rather, the usual message to local leaders is: keep persons with mental illness away from other citizens and families. In this type of environment it is difficult to generate the resources and programs necessary to support programs and services.

TIME-CONSUMING. Collaborative agreements produce relations and actions that are relatively slow because they require equal stakeholder's involvement. If not handled carefully, collaborative agreements can create an environment of increasingly frustrating delays in making a decision on any element of the partnership.

RECIDIVISM. Without adequate programmatic support many persons with mental illness are condemned to living out a seemingly endless cycle of incarceration, return to the community, arrest and re-incarceration. Besides being ineffective this cycle is financially expensive and undermines the role of law enforcement. It is estimated that in many cases we are spending more on this endlessly revolving door than it would cost to properly treat and support the person with mental illness. Ironically, this misallocation of time and money only deepens the problems of the patient and serves as a source of continuing frustration for police and corrections officers.

COURTS. Judges often lack the necessary special training needed in dealing with persons with mental illness. Indeed, persons with mental illness are a bad "fit" to the laws, policies, procedures and processes of most courtrooms. Judges are often ill-equipped to recognize or contend with the issues raised by persons with mental illness. Punishment is an ineffective tool in these circumstances. Yet without viable alternatives judges must either allow charges to stand and follow the legal processes of adjudication or dismiss charges and reactivate the revolving door process. Frequently, judges are not aware of existing treatment resources. In many communities it is essential that efforts to improve communication and coordination between mental health and law enforcement agencies include members of the judiciary. Without their support and involvement it may be impossible to maintain ongoing cooperative programs.

FAMILIES. Many times families who have been through a mental health crisis are hesitant to call the police a second time. They frequently report that they felt that their family member was treated like a criminal and that calling the police would be a betrayal of that person. These feelings sometimes undermine effective support for responding police. They also serve as a basis for criticism of cooperative arrangements between police and local mental health providers. In contrast to supportive families, many families want nothing to do with the person with mental illness. In these instances, family is not there or refuses to provide shelter, transportation or assistance. The burdens of the patient's problems are left to the responding law enforcement agency and the community.

LEGISLATION. Frequently, there are no legislative standards for law enforcement in dealing with persons with mental illness. Thus, there is great variation from community to community and incident to incident in the protocols (or lack of) and processes for dealing with persons with mental illness in crises. Without overarching guidelines and legislation there is little hope of introducing safe and humane consistency into the handling of in-crises persons with mental illness.

Advantages of Collaborative Agreements

In collaborative agreements all stakeholders seek to stimulate and capitalize on a synergetic approach and innovation by catalyzing partnerships among law enforcement, mental health, consumers, advocacy groups, state and local governments, the families and other relevant organizations. Purposes of this collaboration partnership explicitly extend both to developing the personnel, and to creating the necessary organizational conditions to foster the transformation of collaboration into the system and service that fuel prevention development. This creates a new system of interaction with consumers and generates improvements in the national standard of living. The law enforcement institutions that are traditional responders play an essential role in generating new ways of collaboration and creating scientifically approved approaches. Collaborative agreements are an important means for developing the prevention capability of law enforcement and mental health agencies that links integrated services to important societal benefits. Law enforcement agencies can help to redirect efforts of mental health institutions to those areas of the communities that cry for more attention.

Collaborative agreements are advantageous because of the reduction of liability issues that may arise in altercations with the consumers (Minkoff and Pollack, 1997). Nationally sanctioned practices generate fewer lawsuits.

Improving the delivery of mental health services means redressing the imbalances of the past, while focusing on meeting the needs of those who find themselves in a "revolving door" situation. Improving service delivery also calls for a shift away from inward-looking, bureaucratic systems, processes and attitudes, and a search for new ways of working which put the needs of the consumers first. Similar to that of other professions, the continuing growth and professional development of mental health responders may be substantially enhanced by opportunities to collaborate with others. The opportunity to take advantage of the knowledge and expertise of others, and be recognized for their own, can provide mental health responders with important reinforcement and incentive for continuing growth and development, as well as the enhanced personal status and respect that comes from membership in a collaborative entity with their professional colleagues. Professional development will be likely to focus on issues such as developing new responder's functions and organizational structures, establishing collaborative relationships, and helping designated staff consider new ways of utilizing personnel, time, space, and other agency's and community resources. Responding to the new realities requires that responders and administrators develop new information and conceptual understandings related to the changing goals and expectations for mental health services. This collaboration approach also allows the development of local expertise, and capitalizes upon collective experience in ways that would otherwise not be possible. These ways include opportunities to observe others modeling desired services, to benefit from mentoring by partners, and to receive meaningful feedback on their progress. Changing attitudes and expectations are among the most difficult aspects of any professional development experience. Most often these can be changed by opportunities to engage in continuing interaction with other responders who share similar roles, and responsibilities, but who approach them from different perspectives. Collaborative agreements are opening access to "expert systems" for support in decision-making and problem solving through improved communication.

One of the most obvious benefits associated with collaborative agreements is its elimination of duplication in management and services levels. This is due to the high level of agency integration, which will result as various stakeholders' access shared information relevant to their mission and objectives. The increase in agency integration will result in a corresponding decrease in the number of duplicate responses. The elimination of duplicate services is beneficial for several reasons:

- Costs will be reduced.
- Information sharing and integrity will be significantly higher with the elimination of duplicate information systems.
- Costs associated with transportation will be reduced.

Ultimately, however, the primary goal of elimination of duplication is provision of better quality service to consumers.

The Search for Solutions

Law enforcement and mental health agencies should construct a comprehensive collaborative agreement for delivering a broad array of mental health services. Stakeholders should consider the delivery of services at various key points in the criminal justice and mental health systems. The model ideally will involve a high degree of coordination and integration, so that the needs of persons with mental illness are appropriately met as they move through the different levels of the criminal justice and mental health systems.

It should be kept in mind that the ultimate goal of providing services is to reintegrate the person with mental illness back into the community and ensure that he or she becomes a healthy, productive, and successful member of society. Possible long-term solutions can be implemented through the development of synergistically integrated efforts built with the participation of all stakeholders. Obvious short-term solutions are the development of effective intervention techniques; community engagement, and filling gaps in current services for persons with mental illness (shelters, outreach programs, social workers, etc).

A statement of the goals and objectives of the service to be offered through a collaborative arrangement gives a definition and focus of service. There should be a written and legally binding agreement or contract setting out the responsibilities of the stakeholders involved, signed by the heads of the collaborating agencies or groups. Agreements between stakeholders should detail the structure of collaboration, joint protocols and regulations, duration of the agreement, methods of service evaluation, personnel, resource and information sharing arrangements. Each stakeholder should have the right to terminate a written agreement with an agreed period of notice. Responsibilities for the services, protocols and management should be clearly defined. This may include the establishment of a joint committee, which includes representatives from all participating stakeholders. Implementation of a committee's protocols and decisions should be the responsibility of a coordinator. Financial aspects of an agreement should satisfy any agency's funding requirements. There should be adequate safeguards against financial temptations to compromise service standards. Collaborative agreements should be subject to review after an agreed period, and arrangements for review should be determined by all the stakeholders. All publicity material should contain full details of the collaborative agreement. Provision of and control over the accuracy of all public information relating to services should be agreed. Provision should be made for accountability for the quality and standard of all services offered and made under the collaborative agreement. Collaborating agencies should consider how the protocols, rules, and regulations of participating stakeholders should be applied. It is natural that regulations may differ between agencies and that unification of protocols is desirable.

Regional cooperative ventures need to provide service and support to individuals in mental crisis through following stages of contact with mentally ill persons in crisis:

- Information sharing, screening
- Initial contact with law enforcement
- Diversion from the jail
- Pretrial arrangements and adjudication
- Sentencing

- Incarceration
- Transition to community

It is indicated that a mental health information strategy should be created which supports the partnership between law enforcement, mental health providers, consumers, the community, and families. Future information systems and services must meet the needs of both mental health service professionals and law enforcement personnel. The following principles should be utilized in the development of the information-sharing model:

- It should place a priority on the protection of consumer's rights and clearly indicate that the release of information from the consumer's mental health institution to law enforcement personnel requires consumer consent.
- Information should be mental health-criminal justice user based and focused on care of and service for the person with mental illness.
- Stakeholders must provide essential information to the joint unit to support consistent and integrated unit policies and decisions.
- Units should conform to national guidelines and protocols concerning confidentiality of sharing information.
- Units have to respond to all 911 dispatched "emotionally disturbed calls" within their area of jurisdiction at all times.
- There should be notification of mental health agencies of incarceration of mentally ill individuals.
- There should be a state shared communication system.

Implementation of the action plan will require some legislation initiatives. This will involve:

- Lobbying legislators so they understand that problems will get worse–especially in the criminal justice area.
- Seeking statewide standards for transportation, detention, and discharge of persons with mental illness.
- Lobbing legislators to support statewide grants, and other sources of funding, and possibly redirection of existing funding.
- Change certain confidentiality policies for collateral safety.

- Seeking legislative support for statewide recommendations on information sharing.

Conclusion

Increasingly, law enforcement agencies and mental health providers are beginning to recognize the value of collaboration and combining resources to respond in an improved way to consumer and community concerns. The collaborative agreements and initiatives highlighted in this chapter represent important steps toward bridging the gaps between the law enforcement and mental health agencies–gaps through which too many consumers have fallen. Developed state or local collaborations between law enforcement and mental health providers are still relatively few in number, but they are building a very important foundation for future. Criminal justice and mental health communities are beginning to recognize the profound impact of collaboration on mental health crisis survivors and their families and the need for integrated services. The collaborative agreement approach tends to be preventive in nature, which has an impact on a wide range of issues including homelessness, substance abuse, sexual abuse and exploitation, domestic violence, community enhancement, families' well-being, and so on. It is critical to overcome the resistance which still exists on both sides.

REFERENCES

Affeldt, S. (2000). Society as a way of life: Perfectibility, self-transformation, and the origination of society in Rousseau. Monist, 83(4). Available online at http://web3.epnet.com/citation.asp?tb=1&ug=dbs

American Bar Association. (1984). *Criminal justice mental health standards.* Chicago: Author.

Aarons, B. (2000). Mental health and criminal justice. Testimony at Department of Health & Human Services. Available online at www.os.dhhs.gov/asl/testify/t000921a.html

Cohen, A., & Eastman, N. (2000). *Assessing forensic mental health need: Policy, theory and research.* London: Gaskell.

Criminal Justice/Mental Health Consensus Project. (2002). Fact sheet. Available online at http://consensusproject.org/general/about-problem

Deane, M., Steadman, H., Borum, R., Veysey, B., & Morrissey, J. (1999, January). Emerging partnerships between mental health and law enforcement. *Psychiatric*

Services, 50, 99–101.

Finn, P., & Sullivan, M. (1987). *Police response to special populations.* Washington, DC: U.S. Deptartment of Justice, National Institute of Justice, Office of Communication and Research Utilization.

Gerdes, J., Yuen, E., Wood, G., & Frey, C. (2001). Assessing collaboration with mental health providers: The primary care perspective. *Families, Systems & Health, 19,* 4.

Jenkins, R.;McCulloch, A.;Friedli, L.; Parker, C. *Developing a national mental health policy.* Hove: Psychology Press; 2002.

Joint Committee on Mental Health Reform. *A report of the public hearings and findings and recommendations pursuant to senate concurrent resolution No. 59, Chapter 17, Statutes of 2000.* Available online at http://ca.nami.org/cmiterep.htm

Joint Committee on Human Rights. (2004). *3rd Report of Session 2004–05. Deaths in custody.* London: House of Lords, The Stationery Office.

Jurkanin, T. J., Sergevnin, V.A., & Bender, L. G. (2003). *White paper. Modernizing mental health and law enforcement traditional collaboration: Health and enforcing law providers (HELP) units.* Springfield, IL: Illinois Law Enforcement Training and Standards Board Executive Institute.

Karban, K., & Fawcett, B. (2005). *Contemporary mental health: Theory, policy, and practice.* London: Routledge.

Lamb, H. R., Weinberger, L., & DeCuir, W. J. (2002). The police and mental health. *Psychiatric Services, 53*(10), 1266–1271.

Landsberg, G. (2002). *Serving mentally ill offenders: Challenges and opportunities for mental health professionals.* New York: Springer Publishing.

Lavender, A. (2002). Developing services for people with dangerous and severe personality disorders. *Criminal Behavior and Mental Health, 12,* 46–53.

Los Angeles Police Department. (2002). Consent Decree Mental Illness Project Recommendations. Available online at www.lapdonline.org/pdf_files/boi/consent_decree_mental_ill_supp_rpt.pdf

Marans, S. (1995). *The police-mental health partnership.* New Haven, CT: Yale University Press.

Margolis, G. (2002, June 11). Criminal justice system and the mentally ill. FDCH Congressional Testimony. Available online at http://web14.epnet.com/citation.asp?tb

Mental Health Act Commission. (2006). *In place of fear?: Mental Health Act.* London: The Stationery Office.

Mental Health Information Strategy. (2001, March). Department of Health. Available online at www.doh.gov.uk/ipu/whatnew/mhis/mhisdoc2.htm

Mentally Ill Offender Treatment and Crime Reduction Act of 2003. Committee on the Judiciary. Stanford University.

Minkoff, K., & Pollack, D. (1997). *Managed mental health care in the public sector: A survival manual.* London: Routledge.

Reid, W., & Silver, S. B. (2002). *Handbook of mental health administration and management.* Hove, UK: Psychology Press.

Rinehart, T., Laszlo, A., & Briscoe, G. (2002). *Collaboration toolkit: How to build, fix, and sustain productive partnerships.* Washington, DC: Community Oriented Policing Services, U.S. Department of Justice.

Roberts, A. (2005). *Crisis intervention handbook: Assessment, treatment and research* (3rd ed.). New York: Oxford University Press.

Rousseau, J. J. (1762). The social contract or the principles of political. Translated by G.D.H. Cole, Public Domain. Available online at www.constitution.org/jir/socon.htm

Scott, C., & Gerbasi, J. B. (2005). *Handbook of correctional mental health.* Washington, DC: American Psychiatric Publishing, Inc.

Siegel, L. (1990). *American justice: Research of the National Institute of Justice.* St. Paul, MN: West.

Steadman, H., Deane, M., Borum, R., & Morrissey, J. (2000, May). Comparing outcomes of major models of police responses to mental health emergencies. *Psychiatric Services, 51,* 641–649.

Webster's Encyclopedia Unabridged Dictionary of the English Language. (1996). New York: Gramercy Books.

White, V., & Harris, J. (2001). *Developing good practice in community care: Partnership and participation.* London: Jessica Kingsley Publishers.

Chapter 9

A COMMUNITY POLICING APPROACH

GARY W. CORDNER

Encounters with persons with mental illness have long posed a significant challenge for police, and have become commonplace since the advent of deinstitutionalization. Standard responses to this challenge have included better training for general patrol officers and, in larger police departments, the deployment of specialist officers or teams. A full-fledged community policing approach might offer greater potential than these limited "professional model" remedies for improving services and avoiding use-of-force tragedies. This community policing approach emphasizes a broad conception of the police role, personal service, positive interaction, collaboration, partnerships, prevention, and problem solving and relies primarily upon generalist officers permanently assigned to neighborhoods.

Historical Perspective

Long before the police came to be seen principally as crime fighters and crime investigators, they were busy "keeping the peace"–that is, maintaining order, quelling disputes, quieting noise, clearing the streets, and so forth. This fundamental mission has always had a strong urban flavor, and had much to do with the seamier side of the industrial revolution. When factories and commerce attracted thousands of people from the countryside to the city, and later from Europe to America, those who moved were literally uprooted people. Consequently, cities and towns experienced homelessness, unsupervised children, immigrants, and others in desperate straits. They also filled with lots of people who had, for the first time, wage-paying jobs, and thus money to spend on entertainment, including liquor, gambling, and other vices. Amidst this turbulence, concern grew about dangerous elements and dangerous classes, representing a witch's brew of ethnic, racial, economic, and political animosities and specific fears of unions, strikes, and riots (Silver, 1967). Working-class people and propertied elites alike turned to the police as the primary instrument for keeping the peace in such messy times. They still do.

Undoubtedly, within this primary police mission of peacekeeping have always lurked police encounters with persons with mental illness (Bittner, 1967). Prior to deinstitutionalization and the due process revolution in the courts, police had at least three handy alternatives when they encountered a person whose behavior was unpredictable, unexplained, or extreme: (1) they could arrest, jail, and charge the person with disorderly conduct or disturbing the peace; (2) they could detain the person overnight, but then release them without charge; or (3) they could involuntarily commit the person to a mental institution of some sort. These were pretty powerful alternatives that served the police (if not their "clients") rather well. However, option 2 eventually fell into disfavor with the courts and option 3 became much more difficult after deinstitutionalization (Wachholz and Mullaly, 1993). The use of option 1 has been constrained as well, mainly because jailers have become more conscious of civil liability risks and less willing to accept every person the police arrest, regardless of their condition.

Thus, the modern dilemma. The public still expects the police to keep the peace, and with 9/11 the police are more accessible than ever. Also, thanks to deinstitutionalization, more persons with mental illness are in the community, rather than in institutions, therefore increasing the likelihood of encounters with the police, but the options available to the police are now quite limited.

Contemporary Issues

From the general standpoint of police reform and the improvement of police performance, that is, in terms of major police issues in the new millennium, encounters with persons with mental illness fit into three key categories of larger concern. One is simply quality service–police departments and their communities want all kinds of incidents and encounters to be dealt with legally, equitably, and effectively.

From this perspective, encounters with persons with mental illness represent a very complicated situation, as they call for advanced knowledge and skills and since the options available to police officers are significantly constrained (Ruiz, 1993). Put simply, it is a challenge to figure out the right thing to do, to get the person with mental illness to comply, and to get the legal and psychiatric communities to cooperate.

A second general category into which this particular issue fits is our continuing desire to structure police discretion and limit "the overreach of the criminal law." Given deinstitutionalization, the simplest option available to a police officer encountering someone whose behavior is unusual and disturbing is to arrest the person for disorderly conduct. If the officer can get the jail to accept custody of the arrested person, then the officer's immediate problem (and the complainant's, if the officer was responding to a call) is over. However, neither the jail nor the courts really want to see persons with mental illness arrested, detained, and tried. Nor do mental health professionals or police officials. For that matter, the public would probably agree in principle that the criminal law is the wrong tool for such situations. But the reality is that the criminal law sometimes seems like the only option, or at least the only viable option, and therefore it continues to get abused when police encounter persons with mental illness (Gillig, Dumaine, Stammer, Hillard, and Grubb, 1990).

Third, and perhaps most significantly, the specific issue of police encounters with persons with mental illness intersects with the crucial general concern about police use of force. A fundamental element of the police function is the authority to use "non-negotiably coercive force employed in accordance with the dictates of an intuitive grasp of situational exigencies" (Bittner, 1970:46). For all our commitment to policing by consent and our acknowledgment of the historical peacekeeping mission of police work, "everybody knows" that we call the police, in part, when everything else has failed, and when force may be required, up to and including deadly force. Although questions of reasonableness are often raised in the aftermath of incidents of police use of force, particularly deadly force, few question the necessity of this aspect of police authority or the inevitability of its use.

Unfortunately, the police license and capability to use force is often brought into play during encounters with persons with mental illness.

For example, between 1994 and 1999, officers of the Los Angeles Police Department shot 37 people and killed 25 in such encounters (Meyer and Berry 1999). Because the behavior of persons with mental illness is sometimes unpredictable and threatening, it often stimulates forceful responses from officers. Furthermore, initial actions by officers, in the form of verbal commands, may be particularly ineffective with persons with mental illness, thus making escalated police responses even more likely (Fyfe, 2000).

Professional Model Remedies

What modern thinkers call the "professional model" of policing, exemplified by the best aspects of the 1950s and 1960s era popular images of the FBI and the LAPD, held sway over police reform for most of the twentieth century (Kelling and Moore, 1988). Fundamentally, this model emphasized the central role of professional expertise in establishing police legitimacy and achieving efficiency and effectiveness. On a practical level, the professional model relied on such devices as employment standards, training, paramilitary organization, the law, and technology as its principal means of improving police performance and limiting abuses of police authority.

The professional model offers two primary remedies to improve police handling of persons with mental illness–training and specialization (Borum, 2000). The rationale behind training is that police officers can improve their performance in this area if they have more knowledge and/or better skills. Over the past 10–20 years, many police departments and police academies have implemented enhanced training with respect to encounters with persons with mental illness, supported by state-level and national-level mandates and curricula (Murphy, 1986; PERF, 1997). However, this training tends to be relatively brief and represents a minuscule portion of overall police training (Meyer and Berry, 1999). Given the tremendously wide range of social issues that the police must know about, and the extremely diverse set of activities that police perform, it may be naive to expect every police officer to become an expert about mental illness, a skilled counselor, or even just a competent field worker.

Because of this daunting challenge facing the generalist patrol officer, some police departments have attempted to develop specialist officers and/or teams that either provide an immediate response to encounters with persons with mental illness or that provide prompt support to regular patrol officers engaged in such encounters (Turnbaugh, 1999; Dupont and Cochran, 2000). The rationale behind this approach is that a few officers can develop expertise in handling persons with mental illness, if they have special training and if they then practice their skills and use their knowledge regularly. This approach becomes even more powerful if these specialist officers are teamed with mental health professionals. Realistically, though, this approach is probably limited to relatively large police departments that can justify this type of specialization, that have a sufficient volume of encounters such that specialist officers can hone and maintain their skills, and that have mental health professionals near at hand. This should be true for most larger agencies in metropolitan areas, but not for the vast majority of U.S. police departments, which have 25 or fewer sworn employees.

Beyond these two basic approaches–training and specialization–some other specific professional-model remedies have potential for improving police handling of persons with mental illness. One is improved police data and information systems. A study in Lexington, Kentucky revealed that neither the police department's nor the fire department EMS data system captured reliable information about calls and encounters involving persons with mental illness (a characteristic not restricted to this one city), making it very difficult to conduct useful analyses (Biebel and Cordner, 2003). Moreover, these systems did not capture or store information about individual chronic "clients," thus denying patrol officers any opportunity to be notified that the person they have encountered on the street, or the subject of the call to which they are responding, has a mental health-related history with the police department.

While storage of such information raises obvious privacy concerns, officers in Lexington indicated that they wished it was available. They reported that, absent such information from the organization's systems, knowledge about chronic mental health clients was fragmented among individual officers. As a result, the particular patrol officer encountering a subject experiencing a mental health emergency often operated in a vacuum, even though five or ten other officers in the agency "knew all about" the subject and his behavior. This situation particularly affects younger patrol officers, of course, who in turn tend to be disproportionately assigned to evening and night shifts in many departments, when call loads are highest.

Developments in less-than-lethal (LTL) weaponry also have potential to improve police handling of persons with mental illness, by reducing the level of force used by the police and avoiding shootings and fatalities. One of the challenges in this arena is that, in order for it to be useful and practical, LTL equipment has to be readily available to patrol officers and easy to use. In other words, equipment that is stored back at the station, or even in supervisors' cars, may not get to the scene in time to help an officer confronting a subject with a knife or a subject behaving wildly and violently. For that matter, equipment in the trunk of the officer's patrol car may not be accessible during the encounter, at the moment that the officer realizes it might be needed. For these kinds of reasons, pepper spray, which officers can easily carry on their persons, has become the dominant new LTL technology of the past decade (Kaminski, Edwards, and Johnson, 1998). Studies of its effectiveness in specific encounters are promising, but the degree to which it has reduced the overall number of police shootings, if at all, is unknown. It may be that the availability and use of pepper spray has reduced police use of batons, flashlights, and strenuous holds, and reduced the need for police to wrestle with and fight subjects, more than it has reduced police shootings.

One particular aspect of the professional model that has interfered with effective police handling of mental health issues is its tendency to adopt the legalistic style of policing. The professional model has tended to emphasize enforcement of the law as the primary means of policing, and crime fighting as its primary goal. This has caused police to devalue aspects of their job that are not clearly crime-related, such as handling mental health crises. It has also encouraged police to employ enforcement methods as often as possible, leading to arrests of persons experiencing mental health problems when other alternatives would probably be more appropriate.

A related phenomenon that has also been detrimental to effective police work vis-à-vis persons with mental health problems has been the emphasis on officer safety over the last 20 years. More than in previous eras, police training now stresses the threats that police officers can encounter, and teaches officers to respond to those threats in such a way that the officer's own safety is paramount. This might seem like an obvious principle, but it places officer safety on a higher plateau than suspect safety or even the safety of bystanders. It leads to such responses as police use of firearms to counter suspects wielding knives, based on the fact that a knife can cause serious injury or death to the officer. Knives can kill, of course, but the stress on officer safety seems to have created situations in which officers fail to exhaust all other options before resorting to deadly force. These kinds of situations often involve persons with mental illness–persons who seem quite menacing and threatening, but who actually represent little danger if dealt with properly.

A Community Policing Approach

The dominant reform strategy in policing over the last 10–20 years has been community policing. This strategy builds upon the professional model of policing, but gives greater importance to a broader conception of the police role, personal service, positive interaction, partnerships, problem solving, and prevention. The imagery is one of "police and communities working together to solve problems and prevent crime and disorder." Some of the most visible and common ways of operationalizing community policing include foot patrol, bike patrol, mini-stations, neighborhood watch, and school-based programs. At its best, though, community policing represents a more far-reaching reform agenda with philosophical, strategic, tactical, and organizational dimensions (Cordner, 1999).

A broader conception of the police role is crucial to improved police handling of persons with mental illness. If officers regard their role as simply law enforcement and crime fighting, then dealing with a mental health crisis can only be seen as a distraction (not real police work) to be handled as quickly as possible, preferably with an arrest. However, if police recognize that their role has always included (and of necessity must include) resolving conflicts, helping those in danger of harm, and helping those who cannot help themselves, then dealing with a mental health emergency takes on an entirely different complexion. It *is* real police work, and the most effective way of doing it is whatever way best resolves the conflict and helps the person who needs help.

The personal service and positive interaction elements of community policing emphasize that the police are most effective when they maximize their positive interactions with the public, and that the public craves personal service from its government, including its police, rather than impersonal or bureaucratic service. Engaging in proactive positive interactions with the public helps officers tremendously in getting to know the people on their beats, including the people who cause occasional or chronic problems. Such interactions would enable an officer to know by sight and by name the homeless people and panhandlers on her beat, and even to know their stories, all of which would help the officer in both managing their behavior on a day-to-day basis and responding to a crisis or complaint. Similarly, the officer who responds to a mental health-related call in a private home and takes the time to learn something about the individual and their family will be much better prepared the next time they call for help.

The partnership element of community policing also has direct applicability to police handling of persons with mental illness. On an operational level, when police are able to develop collaborative relationships with judicial and mental health professionals, including hospital emergency centers and state hospitals, the often complicated and time-consuming processes for emergency mental health assessments, voluntary commitments, and involuntary commitments can be streamlined and breakdowns in the system can be identified, discussed, and resolved. This can go a long way toward easing police officers' complaints about unsympathetic medical personnel and about having to "babysit" persons experiencing mental health crises for hours and hours. (Note: partnerships and collaboration are discussed in more depth in other chapters of this book.)

Ideally, police departments could develop even more substantive partnerships with concerned local groups such as NAMI chapters. This kind of partnership would embody more of the spirit of community policing. Instead of just working with others in "the system" to enhance its efficiency, this type of partnership would bring the police together with persons with mental illness, family members, advocates, and professionals to work on the whole issue and develop responses that emphasize crisis intervention and prevention and that balance the interests of everyone involved (Turnbaugh, 1999). This approach would place the police into more of an advocacy role, which obviously entails some political risk. However, progressive police executives have long maintained that police have an obligation to take a leadership role with respect to social issues and to speak up on behalf of disenfranchised and stigmatized groups (Sherman, 1985).

Another basic element of community policing that is pertinent to police handling of persons with mental illness is problem solving. This element of community policing should not be confused with crisis intervention or conflict resolution. In the police vernacular, problem solving refers to an effort to look beyond individual incidents (calls, arrests, encounters, etc.) in search of the underlying issues and conditions (i.e., problems) that generate the incidents. Multiple calls to one address might signal an underlying problem, as might a pattern of crimes in a neighborhood or across the city. When a problem is identified, the problem-solving approach then calls for careful analysis, an uninhibited search for tailor-made responses, and careful evaluation to determine whether further action is needed (Goldstein, 1990).

In many ways, police problem solving mimics the public health approach to disease, attempting to deal with causes rather than symptoms. Police are quick to point out, though, that the underlying causes of crime and disorder (poverty, substance abuse, etc.) are beyond their reach. In fact, the problem-solving approach tends to focus on middle-range conditions rather than root causes. When dealing with convenience store robberies, for example, the approach might look at the stores' money handling systems, their physical design, their hours of operation, their staffing levels, and so forth.

One avenue taken in a problem-solving project focused on police handling of persons with mental illness in Lexington, Kentucky was to search for locations where these "problems" were concentrated (Perkins, Cordner, and Scarborough, 1999; also see the "Realistic Expectations of Police" chapter in this book). Although the effort was hampered by data limitations as noted earlier, some interesting findings emerged. Not surprisingly, two hospital trauma centers that handled mental health emergency cases generated numerous calls to the police, as did a state hospital in the city, two homeless shelters, and three boarding homes. The suggestion was made that the police department ought to sit down with officials from each of these facilities (separately) to see whether tailor-made responses could reduce the number of mental health-related calls to the police.

Similarly, ten apartment buildings in Lexington were found to have generated at least three calls each during one year that were determined to be mental health-related. The suspicion that these calls represented just the tip of the iceberg was confirmed in at least one case, that of an apartment building that had logged six "official" calls, but which was found to have generated 33 total calls of a varied nature just from one chronic complainant known to suffer from mental illness. In a situation such as this, the suggestion would be to contact this chronic complainant, his landlord, and his caregivers in an effort to change his behavior and thus prevent, or at least reduce, future unfounded calls to the police department.

Besides taking a broad view of the police role, delivering personal service, seeking positive interactions, working together (collaboration and partnerships) and working smarter (problem solving), community policing has one other element that might contribute positively to police handling of persons with mental illness. Community policing tries to focus police attention on manageable-sized areas of geographic responsibility. In large measure, this boils down to assigning patrol officers more-or-less permanently to neighborhoods. Such permanent assignments are designed to increase police officers' knowledge of, and sense of identification with, the neighborhoods in which they work, and concurrently to enable neighborhood residents to identify "their" officer.

In many respects, this represents an effort by urban police to recapture some of the natural advantages of small town policing. I can testify to these advantages as they relate to encounters with persons with mental illness. While serving as police chief in the small town of St. Michaels, Maryland (population 1,300), I responded to a disturbance call one night and discovered a young woman brandishing a butcher knife. She was threatening everyone in general, but no one in particular, and seemed to be upset and distraught. Although she made some comments about harming herself, and some half-hearted gestures in my direction, a state trooper and I were able to talk her into dropping her knife within about ten minutes. It helped immeasurably that I knew who she was, had dealt with her before in a variety of situations, and knew that she was given to "episodes." Although I had no idea what her clinical condition was, I was pretty confident that she meant me no harm, and I never came close to using force to subdue her.

In another instance, I took a man into custody for threatening and disorderly conduct in and around a church. He immediately became docile, but also completely noncommunicative. I suspected that there was a mental health basis for his behavior, but I didn't know who he was and he carried no identification. Stumped, I took him to jail, where fortunately a deputy sheriff thought he recognized him, and a few phone calls later we had him identified and had contacted his family. Unfortunately, the family refused to come to his aid, but we were able to get some information about his condition and then initiate the mental health assessment and commitment process. In this case, the man would probably have been jailed and prosecuted, but for the local knowledge provided by the deputy sheriff.

These "Andy of Mayberry" experiences of mine illustrate, I think, some of the advantages that can accrue from community policing, even in big cities. Recognizing the breadth of the police role helps legitimize mental health emergencies as "real police work" and validates nonenforcement responses aimed at resolving problems nonviolently. Emphasizing the importance of personal service and positive interactions helps get officers in the frame of mind for providing quality service and helping those in need or in danger of harm, and when officers get to know their assigned neighborhoods and the residents thereof, they gain an advantage. More frequently than otherwise, they know something about the people they encounter. This knowledge helps them diagnose situations more accurately, choose more appropriate dispositions, and judge whether force needs to be used. With respect to persons with mental illness, a patrol officer's familiarity with particular individuals, their families, and their neighbors can make a big difference in how situations are handled.

If we take this line of reasoning one step farther, it might be reasonable to expect that a permanently-assigned beat officer would make a point of being familiar with any of her constituents who have chronic mental health problems, including knowing where they live and work. This beat officer might even check in on such persons periodically, or check with family members and neighbors. Similarly, beat officers might make periodic visits to group homes, homeless shelters, and the like.

Needless to say, this kind of proactive policing raises privacy issues. Unless a person with mental illness is under some type of court jurisdiction, police might lack any legal basis for checking on them, and such police visits might not be welcomed by clients themselves, advocates, or family members. Police and others would need to meet together to decide where to draw the line on obtrusive and invasive police initiatives. In general, though, it would seem to be in everyone's best interests for beat patrol officers to be as familiar as possible with persons likely to experience mental health emergencies, in order to enhance both prevention and effective intervention.

Conclusion

Realistically, big city patrol officers are unlikely to enjoy the degree of familiarity with their constituents that Sheriff Andy enjoyed in Mayberry and that I enjoyed in St. Michaels. Anything that increases their knowledge about their beats and residents, though, such as permanent beat assignment, should improve their ability to respond in a measured and appropriate manner during mental health emergencies, as well as to initiate reasonable problem solving and prevention efforts. Handling of persons with mental illness, like many other aspects of modern policing, is done best by officers who know something about such persons and their situations. We should be striving to achieve a more personal style of policing, rather than the stranger style that long dominated both the image and the reality of American policing.

REFERENCES

Biebel, E. P., & Cordner, G. W. (2003). Repeat calls for people with mental illness: An application of hot spots analysis. *Police Forum, 13*(3), 1–8.

Bittner, E. (1967). Police discretion in emergency apprehension of mentally ill persons. *Social Problems, 15,* 278–292.

Bittner, E. (1970). *The functions of the police in modern society.* Chevy Chase, MD: National Institute of Mental Health.

Borum, R. (2000). Improving high risk encounters between people with mental illness and the police. *Journal of the American Academy of Psychiatry and the Law, 28*(3), 332–337.

Cordner, G. W. (1999). Elements of community policing. In L. K. Gaines & G. W. Cordner (Eds.), *Policing perspectives: An anthology* (pp. 137–149). Los Angeles: Roxbury.

Dupont, R., & Cochran, S. (2000). Police response to mental health emergencies–Barriers to change. *Journal of the American Academy of Psychiatry and the Law, 28*(3), 338–344.

Fyfe, J. J. (2000). Policing the emotionally disturbed. *Journal of the American Academy of Psychiatry and the Law, 28*(3), 345–347.

Gillig, P. M., Dumaine, M., Stammer, J.W., Hillard, J. R., & Grubb, P. (1990). What do police officers really want from the mental health system? *Hospital and Community Psychiatry, 41*(6), 663–665.

Goldstein, H. (1990). *Problem-oriented policing.* New York: McGraw-Hill.

Kaminski. R. J., Edwards, S. M., & Johnson, J. W. (1998). The deterrent effects of oleoresin capsicum on assaults against police: Testing the velcro-effect hypothesis. *Police Quarterly, 1*(2), 1–20.

Kelling, G. L., & Moore, M. H. (1988). The evolving strategy of policing. *Perspectives on Policing No. 4.* Washington, DC: National Institute of Justice.

Meyer, J., & Berry, S. (1999, November 8). Lack of training blamed in slayings of mentally ill. *Los Angeles Times,* pp. A1, A19.

Murphy, G. R. (1986). *Improving the police response to the mentally disabled.* Washington, DC: Police Executive Research Forum.

Nijhar, P., & Brogden, M. (2005). *Community policing: National and international models and approaches.* Portland, OR: Willan Publishing.

Police Executive Research Forum. (1997). *The police response to people with mental illnesses.* Washington, DC: Author.

Perkins, E. B., Cordner, F.W., & Scarborough, K. E. (1999). Police handling of people with mental illness. In L. K. Gaines & G. W. Gordner (Eds.), *Policing perspectives: An anthology* (pp. 289–297). Los Angeles: Roxbury.

Ruiz, J. (1993) An interactive analysis between uniformed law enforcement officers and the mentally ill. *American Journal of Police, 12*(4), 149–177.

Sherman, L.W. (1983). The police executive as statesman. In W. Geller & W. Kerstetter (Eds.), *Police professionalism* (pp. 459–466). New York: Praeger and American Bar Foundation.

Silver, A. (1967). The demand for order in civil society: A review of some themes in the history of urban crime, police, and riots. In D. Bordua (Ed.), *The police: Six sociological essays* (pp. 1–24). New York: John Wiley & Sons.

Turnbaugh, D. G. (1999, October/November). Crisis intervention teams: Curing police problems with people with mental illnesses. *NAMI Advocate,* 11–12.

Wachholz, S., & Mullaly, R. (1993). Policing the deinstitutionalized mentally ill: Toward an understanding of its function. *Crime, Law, and Social Change, 19,* 281–300.

Chapter 10

CREATING EFFECTIVE LAW ENFORCEMENT AND MENTAL HEALTH PARTNERSHIPS

LEWIS G. BENDER

INTRODUCTION

In previous chapters we have focused on the shared problems and issues facing community law enforcement and mental health professionals. In addition, we have identified several of the successful joint responses which have been developed in different communities to address the ongoing needs of mentally ill persons in crisis and the officers who must respond to those persons.

This concluding chapter focuses on ideas and methods of how to create successful collaborative partnerships between local law enforcement agencies, community mental health agencies and relevant stakeholders from the community. Each community is unique. There is no pretense that there is a one-size fits all model of partnership that will work with all police departments or community mental health agencies. Rather the purpose of this chapter is to:

- Identify many of the "cultural" differences between community mental health and law enforcement agencies that must be bridged in order to develop a working partnership.
- Delineate some of the benefits that might occur from forming police/mental health partnerships.
- Identify and discuss lessons from past partnership efforts that may help leaders to improve the chances for creating successful col-

laborations and partnerships between police and mental health agencies.
- Suggest some ideas for starting the collaborative process.

Defining Where We Are Going: Partnerships

The term "partnership" is a widely used and misused term. For the purposes of this discussion we borrow from two mutually supportive definitions.

Rodal and Mulder define a partnership as:

> an arrangement between two or more parties who have agreed to work cooperatively toward shared and/or compatible objectives and in which there is: shared authority and responsibility; joint investment of resources; shared liability or risk taking; and ideally mutual benefits. (Rodal and Mulder, 1993:28)

The concepts identified by Rodal and Mulder are echoed in the operational definition used by the New Economy Development Group in its community-based definition of partnership:

> a relationship in which government and other agents work co-operatively to achieve a . . . goal at the community level. It requires the sharing or resources, responsibilities, decision-making, risks and benefits, according to a mutually agreed-upon formal or informal arrangement. (New Economy Development Group, 1996:16)

These two definitions contain several key elements that must be embraced prior to any attempt to create an effective partnership.

1. *All partners must subscribe to the same set of goals.* If the goals or agendas are radically different the partnership has little chance of success. This frequently means that leaders must spend time together determining what the acceptable and shared objectives will be for the collaborative effort.
2. *Members of the partnership must share the decision-making, responsibility and authority central to the joint enterprise.* "One-way" partnerships inevitably fail. Respective leaders must reach an understanding regarding the roles, responsibilities and authority that will be shared and not shared in the collaborative effort. Subordinates may assist in the efforts to identify key points of shared authority. It is best, however, that organizational leaders

ultimately determine the areas of shared responsibility and authority and not leave these matter to chance.

3. *Members of a partnership must make the same level of commitment to the success of the joint venture.* This means that they should contribute equal resources to the partnership and also share equally in the risks and benefits of the enterprise.

Community law enforcement and mental health leaders need to have a shared understanding of partnership in order to develop an effective working relationship. Sometimes that understanding takes time and multiple meetings to develop. Regardless of the route or the time involved it is essential that all parties have a clear understanding of the shared goals, authority, responsibilities, risks and benefits involved in the partnership.

Farmers speak of to the commitment that a pig brings to the breakfast table compared to the commitment that a chicken brings to the meal. Ultimately, if collaborations are to be effective between law enforcement and mental health agencies, the leaders of those agencies must decide whether they are jointly going to bring the commitment of chickens or pigs to the enterprise. Halfway measures by one party or the other can only lead to failure.

The Strengths and Challenges of Difference: The Cultures of Law Enforcement and Mental Health

The "culture" of an organization or system refers to an "integrated pattern of human knowledge, belief, and behavior" and "the set of shared attitudes, values, goals and practices" which define and characterize human decisions and interactions (Webster, 1996). Even the most cursory examination of the histories, structures, practices and general operations of law enforcement and mental health reveal fundamental and substantial differences. Any attempt to establish short-term collaborations or long-term partnerships must be based on the historical and present realities of each culture. Law enforcement leaders may be particularly confused by the complex and convoluted service model and support systems which have developed within community-based mental health.

Not unlike law enforcement, mental health operations continue to grapple with significant changes in the philosophy and operations of their service. Thirty years ago the mental health profession generally accepted the grim reality that mental illness was chronic and irreversible. With tremendous advances in medications and treatment protocols those grim realities have given way to the combined realities and hopes of recovery for patients. Correspondingly, the approaches to treatment have quickly changed from removing mentally ill people from society and the general population to strategies for integrating patients into the community (Jurkanin and Sergevnin, 2002).

Generally, clinicians, advocates and stakeholders agree that it is preferable to keep patients in the community and avoid long-term hospitalization. Most analysts agree that this shift from hospitalization to community integration has not seen a proportional shift in funding support. Again, mental health practitioners and advocates are in general agreement that this funding lag, as well as other factors, has led to increased failures and breakdowns in treatment for some segments of the population (Criminal Justice 2002:5).

Significant divisions, however, exist within mental health organizations over what to do when community-based systems fail to effectively treat people. The issue of involuntary commitment has been the subject of heated debate among practitioners and stakeholders. One side of the debate sees involuntary commitment as dehumanizing and an extreme measure to be avoided at all costs. Other professionals believe that this is a step that must be utilized as a lifesaving measure when treatment and other interventions fail. This debate within mental health will inevitably be a source of concern in establishing protocols for police and mental health roles in dealing with people in crises.

Law enforcement leaders may find that attempts to create partnerships with various community-based mental health operations may be confusing and frustrating. One operation may be very supportive of many underpinning philosophies of local law enforcement whereas other operations may view police in a hostile manner. In either case, law enforcement leaders should avoid preconceptions and stereotypes regarding the views or receptiveness of community mental health leaders.

Similarly, law enforcement is not a monolithic or static system. As noted in previous chapters, law enforcement has also undergone numerous changes over the past thirty years. The debate continues in many circles over the changing roles and expanding demands upon law enforcement agencies.

Philosophies and programs ranging from community-oriented policing to D.A.R.E.(r) and school liaison operations have challenged and changed the nature and culture of many local law enforcement organizations. Ongoing debates and discussions focus on questions about the role of law enforcement and whether police should be attempting to service different constituencies. Similar to mental health, law enforcement leaders are actively discussing their role and relationship to the community, and similar to mental health leaders, the views of law enforcement leaders and practitioners may be very diverse.

Complex questions of history, philosophy and current practices may significantly impact attempts to create collaborations and partnerships between local law enforcement and community mental health. At the risk of oversimplifying two very complex and dynamic "systems" the following outlines some of the major cultural differences which tend to define community based mental health and local law enforcement operations.

LAW ENFORCEMENT CULTURE	MENTAL HEALTH CULTURE
Practitioner: *Deal with Perpetrators/Victims*	Practitioner: *Serve Patients/Clients*
Practitioner: *Focus on Safety/Protection*	Practitioner: *Focus on Treatment/Health*
Practitioner: *Control/Restrain*	Practitioner: *Help/Assist*
Practitioner: *Short-Term Intervention*	Practitioner: *Long-Term Involvement*
Service Contact: *Immediate Results/Resolution*	Service Contact: *Long-Term/Evolving Changes*
Tools: *Listen/Direct/Take Action*	Tools: *Listen/Empathize/Coach/Prescribe*
Contact Times: *24/7/365*	Contact Times: *Scheduled*
Organization: *Chain of Command*	Organization: *Practitioner Focused*
Public Visibility: *High*	Public Visibility: *Low*
Community Support: *Low to High*	Community Support: *Low*
Funding: *Primarily Local*	Funding: *Federal/State/Local/Patient (Inconsistent)*

These and other cultural differences may have a big impact on the focus of collaborative discussions and the ultimate outcomes of those talks. Greater understanding by law enforcement and mental health leaders of each other's opportunities, constraints and overall realities may eliminate presumption and judgment as defining factors in collaborative discussions. For example, frequently law enforcement leaders may find that they have more flexibility in allocating manpower and funds to new or special initiatives then their mental health counterparts.

The local nature of law enforcement funding is often more flexible than the myriad funding sources which tend to support mental health. An incomplete list of community mental health funding sources includes: "Medicaid, Medicare, state general revenue funds, local matches, federal Mental Health Block Grants (grants administered by three or more federal agencies), patient fees, just to name the most common. In some states, funds are funneled through managed-care frameworks. In others, counties present an additional level of administration" (Criminal Justice 2002:16–17). The inevitable strings attached to mental health funding sources may limit the ability of leaders to immediately develop new programs or realign existing operations.

In spite of the differences in the cultures of mental health and law enforcement, there are areas in which leaders will find some significant similarities. For example, leaders may find mutual commiseration related to the challenges of dealing with the public and communities that send mixed signals regarding the desirability of their services. Police and mental health professionals frequently have been told in one breath that they are greatly (urgently) needed and in another referred to as a necessary and expensive "evil."

The public often expresses ambivalent views of the roles and necessity of police and mental health presence. Similarly, police and mental health professionals are frequently accustomed to critique and second-guessing of their actions. Correspondingly, they are also accustomed to reckoning with the irrationalities of politics and community gamesmanship. Misery does love company. Sometimes leaders who have fought similar battles can find more in common than would be indicated from their dissimilar backgrounds and occupations.

Potential Benefits to Forming Law Enforcement and Mental Health Partnerships

In the final analysis, it may be the perceived and real benefits that cause parties to form and maintain community-based partnerships. Benefits may range from attempting to mitigate a negative situation or string of occurrences to creating positive changes that enhance the welfare of partners and stakeholders. In many cases collaborative talks have commenced because of recent tragedies involving police and mentally ill persons in crises (Lamb, Weinberger, and DeCuir, October 2002).

The impetus in these cases is to address the immediate situation and hopefully create longer-term mutual responses to shared problems and issues. The existence of high visibility crises may be the factor that causes law enforcement and mental health leaders to come together. Immediate crises, however, may not be enough to sustain collaborative talks. Leaders must find other supportive reasons to build and maintain a working partnership.

The Council of State Government's Criminal Justice/Mental Health Consensus Project (2002) identified eight potential benefits of collaborations that may appeal to key local leaders. They include:

- Improve the lives of people with mental illness and reduce the frequency of their contact with the criminal justice system
- Enhance public safety
- Use criminal justice resources more efficiently
- Improve the safety of line staff and of the environment in which they work
- Reduce taxpayer expenditures
- Increase public confidence in the justice system
- Gain access to resources
- Enlist allies capable of attracting support from policymakers previously unmoved by the need to bolster the mental health system (2002:17)

Beyond these benefits it is possible that partnerships involving voluntary organizations and stakeholders such as local chapters of the National Alliance for the Mentally Ill (NAMI) could yield other important side-effects such as improved constituent support when crises occur. When parties are part of the problem-solving process and not excluded they tend to have increased ownership of good and bad outcomes and tend to be less judgmental of prior efforts. This, combined with the links which most voluntary organizations have to the community can be a significant asset during difficult times. Similarly, voluntary leaders have the capability and flexibility to lobby local and state policymakers in a more aggressive and visible manner than mental health and law enforcement leaders. This also could provc to be a major asset as the partnership evolves and grows.

Key leaders may also find that an ongoing relationship will produce mutually useful data that may lead to improved and more efficient processes in each of their operations. By sharing important data and discussing the trends and implications of the information professionals may find better strategies for deploying human and financial resources.

Minimally, during times of crisis, ongoing constructive collaborative talks between law enforcement and mental health leaders might eliminate or reduce tensions and finger pointing between the two sectors. Optimally, collaborative talks may lead to a partnership that is dynamic and is able to address the needs of law enforcement officers and mentally ill persons in crises.

Five Lessons to Be Learned From Past Community-Based Partnerships

The history of community-based collaborations and partnerships is strewn with examples of failed attempts to create alliances between diverse organizations and groups. Experienced facilitators agree that there are numerous factors and variables to consider. Similarly, there isn't a set formula or "cookbook" which can guide community leaders through the myriad shoals and obstacles which can appear suddenly and without warning during the process. Nonetheless, there has been much written on community-based collaborations. Similarly, a great deal of knowledge has been developed by community leaders and those who facilitate community-based partnerships on what to do and not do in forming a partnership. The following five lessons summarize some of the main points raised throughout the literature on the topic of forming effective community-based partnerships.

Lesson 1: One Step at a Time: Build Relationships and Trust

Then Build a Partnership. The saying on the street used to be "speed kills." This most certainly applies to developing effective community-based partnerships. The very notion of creating a partnership means that there will be changes in the way business is done. This often means that leaders must think beyond the present and see things in a larger not yet fully developed context (Kerka, 1997).

The thinking of the past may need to be replaced by a new vision and approach that may challenge previous assumptions. For example, past hostilities or assumptions that may have intensified problems between law enforcement and mental health professionals may have to be replaced with greater understanding of each other's roles and a new vision of mutual support. This kind of transformation does not occur just because leaders think that it is a good idea (Bendle/Carmen-Aisnworth, 1996).

Leaders must spend time with each other developing mutual understanding, vision and trust. The understandings developed at the highest level usually establish the boundaries for the partnership. If there is suspicion and lack of trust at the highest level there will probably be little chance of creating a partnership which is dynamic and responsive to evolving needs. Similarly, if the relationship between leaders is built on mutual understanding and trust the new partnership has a better chance of addressing the inevitable obstacles and growing to meet other shared needs and concerns.

Active involvement by leaders in the early stages of conceptualizing and creating a partnership is essential. Studies indicate that the early active involvement or lack of involvement of key leaders is a major predictor of outcomes in forming partnerships (Berger, 1997). Successful collaboration and partnership require a great deal of work. Collaborators must clearly understand each other and why they are forming a partnership. They must understand and be able to explain to each other and the organizations they lead: why they are forming a partnership. This will be especially true when the challenges and problems which confront all partnerships appear (Hageman et al. 1999).

Clearly, there is no set formula to determine how often or how long leaders should meet in the conceptual and formative stages of a partnership. Perhaps the best indicator is whether participants are comfortable enough with each other to freely and informally discuss issues and concerns in a nondefensive manner. Leaders need to reach the point where they can pick up the phone or informally meet to address individual and mutual concerns.

Lesson 2: Create Clear and Realistic Goals with Appropriate Resource Commitments-Build Early Success. The previous theme of one step at a time in building the early relationship also applies to the process of setting early goals for the partnership. Leaders must create goals which can be accomplished and which allow members of their organizations to develop relationships and trust as they attempt to develop and implement new processes. Even if the leaders of the partnership can agree on a longer-term vision and major goals it is essential that they establish shorter interim goals (Mizrahi, 1999).

By initially establishing goals and objectives that can be accomplished, leaders of the partnership improve the chances of creating a foundation of trust and cooperation as opposed to an environment of frustration, failure and finger pointing. For example, as noted in previous chapters, many law enforcement and mental health agencies begin their partnership by focusing on developing mutual training strategies. The training objectives were "doable" and allowed individuals from both disciplines to share knowledge and information in a nonthreatening way.

This early incremental approach to establishing goals and objectives also increases the chances of greater shared ownership by key members from the respective teams. One early strategy may involve the creation of a small task force comprised of coalition members who are charged with the task of identifying mutual training needs and strategies. This early involvement by mental health and law enforcement personnel could become the base for planning and implementing larger future goals (Hageman et al., 1999). It is much easier to tackle more difficult and involved goals from a base of previous success as opposed to a history of frustration and failure. Leaders of the partnership need to appreciate that their subordinates will encounter a learning curve just as they did in their initial discussions.

Just as there will inevitably be a learning curve for the participants of a partnership there will also be a potential resource-lag curve. In recent times the familiar mantra for both mental health and law enforcement has been "do more with less." This inevitably means that budgets and personnel are stretched and that new initiatives such as forming partnerships must be accomplished by asking people to stretch, yet again, to accomplish worthy objectives. Under these circumstances it becomes imperative that leaders of the partnership develop early goals and objectives which realistically reflect available human and budget resources. Again, the key in the early stages is to create a combination of shared ownership and success by the participants in the partnership.

Lesson 3: Shared Goals Must Always Trump Turf and Territory. A partnership can fail even when the need is great and the idea is wonderful and well-received by important players. In many instances forming a partnership means that past practices have failed and a different approach is needed to address the issues. This sometimes means that the new way of doing business (partnership) may create some new "winners" and "losers." People who feel that they will "lose" in the new arrangement or who are just resistant to change may create a formidable obstacle to the new partnership.

Typically, people vested in the old ways of doing things are better organized and may be politically more potent than the new "winners" who may not yet even be identified. This may be a major challenge to the leaders of the new partnership. If trust and open communication between leaders has not been established, the ability to control recalcitrant subordinates may be very limited.

Beyond the commitment of time and resources by leaders, perhaps the biggest challenges to a new partnership are questions around *turf and territory*. Where do I end and you begin, and what do we do together? These kinds of questions test the commitment and the metal of most new partnerships. Ideally, most of these types of questions need to be addressed by partnership leaders BEFORE involving subordinate staffs in the processes of attempting to accomplish specific goals and objectives. Leaders need to anticipate and explore the boundaries of the partnership. It is not just a matter of how many dollar resources they are willing to commit. The biggest challenges come with committing staff who already are involved in other processes and previous commitments.

Turf and territory are not necessarily negative factors. Indeed, for many employees the identification and pride that comes with an area of responsibility (turf) can be a great source of energy and pride. In this light, turf becomes a positive force for an organization. Employees take care that the job is done thoroughly and in a timely manner because it reflects on them. This positive energy can be the source for great angst and conflict for many employees when they feel that their work is threatened or unappreciated. In this situation, highly-motivated and positive employees can become contrary to the new goals and objectives of the partnership. In these circumstances, protecting turf and territory become more important than accomplishing desired tasks and objectives. Winer and Ray note that this can be avoided if partnerships take into account the current duties of participants. "Most partnerships work best when the partners create a structure that helps members manage the extra work that happens when collaborating begins" (1994: 82). As noted previously, leaders must anticipate and deal with these types of issues. Many times turf issues can be identified ahead of time and proactive steps can be taken to address or mitigate potential problems. In other times leaders will have to consider sanctions and other steps to prevent negative impacts of turf issues. In either scenario it is essential that partnership leaders identify and discuss these issues and that they not allow shared partnership goals to be undermined by turf questions.

Lesson 4: Create Effective Structures and Processes That Move Beyond Current Personalities. Partnerships are primarily horizontal, not vertical structures. They are similar to coalitions in that they essentially are organization of organizations "with a common goal and diverse structures, ideologies, resources, power, and constituencies (Mizrahi, 1999:19). The metaphor of a ladder is instructive of the structure of many partnerships. The vertical side rails represent the distinct hierarchical organizations that comprise the partnership. The rungs of the ladder represent the horizontal connections that must exist between and among partners in order to make the collaboration work. To push the metaphor, if only the top rungs of the ladder are in place the ladder (partnership) will fail. Similarly, it is essential that leaders develop a partnership structure that connects the participant organization's at all key levels. Without these connections (rungs) between various levels of the respective organizations the partnership effort will remain a leadership dependent structure. Typically, when this happens the partnership can only remain viable during the time that leaders can give it priority. In these cases, as other needs and demands redirect the attention of the respective organization leaders the partnership oftentimes fails.

The same trust that was essential for leaders in the early stages of collaboration is equally important for other members of the respective organizations through the ongoing implementation stages. This means that leaders of the partnership need to jointly involve people at all key levels of the partnership effort. Joint task teams need to address critical operational questions and be able to give input regarding the best approaches for achieving relevant objectives. Usually, this means that partnership leaders must avoid dictating specific processes and engage joint task teams with questions and challenges.

For example, partnership leaders might challenge a task group of first-line supervisors in the partner mental health agency and shift commanders from the police department to come up with options for around-the-clock coordination between agencies, or, such a task team might identify key issues that need to be addressed in joint training. Whatever the specific topic, it is essential that members at all key levels of the partnership be involved in mutual problem solving and be responsible for generating ideas and processes that can help the partnership work. Beyond the specific objectives or problems that are addressed, the contacts between organizational partners should encourage communication, understanding and eventually mutual trust.

Eventually, task groups should evolve into ongoing, formally structured contacts between and among members of the partnership. As the partnership moves into an ongoing implementation mode it is essential that regular informal and formal contact be built into the structure of the partnership. It is usually a mistake to only meet when there is a problem or a failure. Partnership members should be charged with scheduled and ongoing contacts that monitor the status of shared operations and that are focused on developing ways to improve processes and even expand objectives. If contact between partnership members is only when something fails or there is a problem, there is a greater likelihood that tensions will increase within the partnership.

It is also important to involve new persons from the partner organizations in the ongoing process. As people move in the organization, or join or leave the partner organizations, it is essential that new people be oriented to the history of the partnership and that they be encouraged/expected to continue the work of the partnership.

Similarly, it is important for leaders to expect the ongoing involvement of numerous members of their organization as opposed to one or two persons. Even when one or two people are more highly motivated to do the tasks and work of the partnership it is essential that others should maintain an active involvement.

If the work of the partnership becomes the "job" of one or two persons, the chances increase that others will not be as committed to its success and/or the success of the partnership will be limited to the personalities of those motivated persons. For example, assignment of the role of coordinator should not be code for "this is your job and the rest of us don't have to think about it." Leaders of the partnership need to take care that numerous people throughout the partner organizations are involved in the ongoing communication and work of the partnership.

Lesson 5: Don't Walk Away. Leaders Must Empower, Monitor and Continue to Support the Partnership. It is not unusual that the involvement and time of partnership leaders will decrease over time. Indeed, as the collaborative efforts grow between partner organizations it is healthy that others have greater involvement in the partnership. Most analysts agree that leaders in the partnership should strive to empower others as part of the normal growth and progression of the partnership (Huxham and Vangen, 2000; Kerka, 1997; Mattessich and Monsey, 1992).

There is also general agreement that empowerment of staff should not translate to disengagement by partnership leaders. Rather, the role of leaders should move to that of regularly monitoring ongoing programs and specifically supporting staff and other engaged operatives. This can be accomplished in numerous ways. Perhaps the most common approach is that leaders schedule regular (quarterly/tri-annually) meetings with each other and key partnership staff operatives to discuss how the partnership is progressing. In these meetings, data may possibly be discussed and analyzed, problems addressed, successes identified and new objectives created. These types of meetings can send a strong signal to members of the partnership that leaders continue to care about the success of the partnership and that they are supportive of the efforts of the respective staffs.

This type of regular monitoring will also permit leaders to continue to build trust with each other. In addition, these regularly scheduled meetings may provide the basis for expanding the partnership into new areas of mutual endeavor.

Some Thoughts and Ideas on Beginning the Collaborative Process

Every person in a leadership role has approaches and strategies that fit their personality and work for them. Thus, there is no one set of suggestions or recommendations related to the collaborative process that could fully apply to all law enforcement or mental health leaders. Nonetheless, experience and the literature indicate that there are some ideas that leaders might ponder during the earliest and most fragile stages of forming a partnership.

Step 1: The first meeting should be in a neutral and comfortable place. Have lunch. The first meeting between leaders should be relaxed, informal and on neutral turf. If possible, avoid any setting that "belongs" to any of the participants. People tend to be less inclined to be open to new ideas if they are in a setting where the old ideas or normal ways of doing business predominate. This is one of the reasons professional facilitators insist on conducting strategic planning meetings at neutral and comfortable locations. Frequently, this encourages participants to be creative and explore new ideas.

Similarly, people who eat together tend to be more comfortable and relaxed. Since the idea of the early meeting between leaders is to explore mutual concerns and a potential partnership, it may serve everyone well to make the early discussion(s) as comfortable and as informal as possible.

Step 2: Keep the initial meetings small. Identify the top key leaders and keep the group small. Three or four people are usually better than seven or eight. In these early stages, the main agenda is to explore ideas, issues and potential relationships. Key leaders should have the opportunity to freely discuss things in an atmosphere that discourages "posturing."

Frequently, larger meetings have the combined effects of encouraging some people to be guarded while others posture. As the discussions evolve, it is always possible to identify and invite others to participate in forming the partnership. Early on, however, the usual best practice is to keep the group small and the discussions informal.

Step 3: Don't "present" problems or ideas, ask and discuss. The initial and early meetings should focus on exploring shared areas of concern and potential consensus. The central purpose is to create a sense of shared ownership of problems, ideas and goals that may lead to commitment to a partnership. Shared ownership of an idea or issue is facilitated by asking nonconfrontational questions and soliciting discussion.

When participants are involved in exploring issues and identifying options, they tend to create a sense of shared ownership over the problems and solutions. If one person attempts to present the problems, options and solutions the other participants tend to view the analysis and answers as his or hers and they tend to not share in the ownership of the outcomes.

Creative problem solving involves four key steps:

1. *Participants identify the problem or goal and reach a consensus regarding causes and effects of the problem/goal.*
2. *Participants discover and explore options and ideas for resolving the problem or achieving the goal. Frequently, this involves brainstorming and weighing of the pros and cons of different strategies and approaches.*
3. *When participants have created a consensus on direction, they form a "contract for implementation" and decide who, what, when, where, and how.*
4. *Participants then monitor and evaluate progress and make appropriate adjustments to the process.*

This is not a totally linear process. Most groups will oscillate between steps one and two before moving to step three. It is during this part of the creative decision process that members of the group begin to learn about each other and develop a sense of shared ownership over the issues and potential solutions. Individuals who are not present during the back and forth discussion around steps one and two oftentimes have trouble "buying-in" to the solutions presented in step three.

Frequently, leaders experience this phenomenon when they identify, discuss and solve problems at the command and management level and find that people in the ranks initially criticize or reject the final decision. Frequently, it is not about whether the decision is right or the best decision. It is about whether key people feel they are a part of the decision process (steps one and two) and thus, whether they have a sense of ownership in the decision.

In the early stages of collaboration, leaders need to create an environment and process that encourages shared ownership of the problems, goals, options and solutions central to the emerging partnership. This is best done if nonthreatening/analytical questions are mutually asked and options are explored together.

Step 4: Recognize and appreciate differences and focus on shared concerns and goals. The process of collaboration requires that leaders be able to distinguish trivial from important issues and differences. Some issues will be more important to certain leaders and members of the forming partnership than others. The ability to understand those areas of differing views of importance is an essential part of the collaborative process. This requires that leaders learn about each other's organizations and develop an appreciation for their respective histories, successes and challenges.

This understanding oftentimes serves as the foundation for identifying shared issues and developing shared goals. Leaders of collaborative efforts who do not have a shared base of understanding and appreciation of key differences frequently get sidetracked into making negative judgments about each other. This becomes counter-productive to the development of trust and the formation of the partnership.

Step 5: Be patient and in a hurry. Clearly this is conflicting advice. Nonetheless, it is good advice. The initial stage of collaboration among potential partners requires time and patience. The agenda at this stage should be the exploration of shared issues and ideas and most importantly the *development of mutual understanding and trust.* As noted previously, this may take many contacts over an extended period of time. During this time it is better if pressure be kept at a minimum. Leaders will need to examine many things on the path to creating mutual trust and consensus.

Once a foundation of understanding, mutual trust and basic consensus has been established, it is important that the tempo of the forming partnership change. The relaxed pace of the early discussions should be replaced with a more urgent pace. The sense of urgency that partnership leaders display to their team members is oftentimes an indicator of level of importance. Thus, if leaders are not in a hurry and don't display a sense of urgency, staff members may view this new initiative as not important or superficial compared to other priorities.

Similarly, if leaders display a sense of urgency and are cognizant of the other priorities facing staff the partnership effort has a better chance of moving along at an acceptable pace.

Conclusion

The demands upon law enforcement and community-based mental health agencies continue to expand. Services that used to be taken care of by families and/or other institutions now, by default, have become the responsibility of the police and mental health professionals. The problems facing our society also continue to expand. For example, most studies estimate that up to 25 percent of single adult homeless persons are seriously mentally ill (Criminal Justice 2002: xiii). The impacts of this and other growing problems will provide the impetus for more creative and integrated approaches to addressing the issues. It is safe to project that the future will require more efforts to form collaborative partnerships in communities throughout the country.

As noted previously, there is no definitive guidebook on forming community-based partnerships. The number of factors that can positively and negatively influence a collaborative effort, let alone a partnership, are too numerous to anticipate. Leaders will need to primarily rely on the knowledge they have gained from past successful and unsuccessful collaborations as well as consult with others and the literature before choosing their collaborative approach. Even then, well-intentioned and experienced leaders can do everything "correctly" and still have the effort to form a partnership fail. The act of leading involves risk and the creation of positive changes for organizations and communities. Inherent in any risk is the potential for failure, as well as the potential for success.

Creating community-based partnerships between two very different types of organizations; law enforcement and community mental health, will involve a certain level of risk for key leaders. Nonetheless, the potential benefits for police officers, persons with mental illness and the community are well worth the risks.

REFERENCES

Bendle/Carmen-Aisnworth Community Schools. (1996). *The learning community. A pro-family system of education and community services.* Flint, MI: The Learning Community.

Berger, A. (1997). *Public leaders and multi-sectional collaborations: Assessing the influence of leaders on partnership outcomes.* Paper presented at the Annual Meeting of the Academy of Management, Boston.

Criminal Justice/Mental Health Consensus Project. (2002). Council of State Governments. Available online at www.concensusproject.org

Hageman, W. M., Harmata, R., Zuckerman, H., Werner, B., Alexander, J., & Bogue, R. (1999). Collaborations that work. *Health Forum Journal, 42*(5), 46–48.

Huxham, C., & Vangen, S. (2000). Leadership in the shaping and implementation of collaboration agendas: How things happen in a (not quite) joined-up world. *Academy of Management Journal, 43*(6), 1159–1175.

Ekos Research Associates. Voluntary Sector Roundtable. (1998). *Lessons learned on partnerships: Final report.* Ottawa, Canada.

Freeman, T., & Peck, E. (2006, September). Evaluating partnerships: A case study of integrated specialist mental health services. *Health & Social Care in the Community, 14*(5), 408–417.

Jurkanin, T. J., & Sergevnin, V. A. (2002). Police training response to mental health crisis. *Law Enforcement Executive Forum, 2*(4), 97–105.

Kerka, S. (1997). *Developing collaborative partnerships.* Practice Applications Briefs, retrieved from ERK Clearinghouse: http://eric.ed.gov/ERICDocs/data/ericdocs2sql/content_storage_01/0000019b/80/16/49/64.pdf (July 12, 2007)

Lamb, R., Weinberger, L., & DeCuir, W. (2002, October). The police and mental health. *Psychiatric Services, 53*(10), 1266–1271.

Mattessich, P. W., & Monsey, B. R. (1992). *Collaboration: What makes it work.* St. Paul, MN: Amherst H. Wilder Foundation.

Merriam Webster's Collegiate Dictionary. (10th ed.) (1996). Springfield, MA: Merriam-Webster, Inc.

Mizrahi, T. (1999). Strategies for effective collaborations in the human services. *Social Policy, 29*(4), 5–20.

New Economy Development Group, Inc. (1996, July). *A study of innovative examples of local partnerships.* Ottawa, Canada: Human Resources Development.

Rodal, A., & Mulder, N. (1993, Winter). Partnerships, devolution and power-sharing: Issues and implications for management, optimum. *The Journal of Public Sector Management, 24*(3), 27–48.

Wells, W., & Schafer, J. A. (2006). Officer perceptions of police responses to persons with a mental illness. *Policing: An International Journal of Police Strategies & Management, 29*(4), 578–601.

Winer, M., & Ray, K. (1994). *Collaboration handbook: Creating, sustaining, and enjoying the journey.* St. Paul, MN: Amherst H. Wilder Foundation.

ABOUT THE AUTHORS

Dr. Thomas J. Jurkanin was appointed as Executive Director of the Illinois Law Enforcement Training and Standards Board on April 1, 1992.

Dr. Jurkanin has been employed by the Board for the past 28 years in various administrative capacities. He has 32 years of work experience in the criminal justice field. Dr. Jurkanin holds a Ph.D. in Education from Southern Illinois University at Carbondale and both the Bachelors and Masters Degree in Social Justice from the University of Illinois at Springfield. Dr. Jurkanin has authored numerous articles and professional papers and is Senior Editor of the *Law Enforcement Executive Forum.* He is co-author of two books entitled, *Enduring, Surviving and Thriving as a Law Enforcement Executive,* and *Critical Issues in Police Discipline: Case Studies* published by Charles C Thomas. Dr. Jurkanin recently authored a book entitled *Chicago Police: An Inside View.*

Dr. Jurkanin is Vice Chairman of the Governor's Law Enforcement Medal of Honor Committee and a member of the Education and Training Committee, International Association of Chiefs of Police. Jurkanin was also the recipient of the 2004 Pastor Paul-Gerhard Braun Award, presented by the National Association of Mental Illness (Illinois), for his outstanding work in developing training models for police to better serve persons with mental illness.

Dr. Larry Hoover received his Ph.D. from Michigan State University, has been on the criminal justice faculty at Sam Houston State University since 1977, and directs its Police Research Center. Dr. Hoover, a past president of the Academy of Criminal Justice Sciences, is the recipient of the Academy's "2003 Founder's Award" as well as the "O. W. Wilson Award" from the its Police Section. He is also the recipient of the "Excellence in Research Award" from SHSU, and was recognized in 2005 by Michigan State University by induction to the School of Criminal Justice "Wall of Fame." His current endeavors include the administration of a statewide police information management system (CRIMES), directing the Texas Law Enforcement Management and Administrative Statistics Program (TELEMASP), presiding over an Executive Issues Seminar Series sponsored by the Law

Enforcement Management Institute of Texas, and managing several grant projects from the National Institute of Justice. He is editor of the anthologies *Police Management: Issues and Perspectives, Quantifying Quality in Policing,* and *Police Program Evaluation,* all published by the Police Executive Research Forum, and coauthor of *Enduring, Surviving, and Thriving As A Law Enforcement Executive,* Charles C Thomas Publisher.

Vladimir Sergevnin, Ph.D. earned a Bachelor of Arts degree from Leningrad Pedagogical University in History and a doctorate of philosophy from the Moscow Institute of National Economy. Dr. Sergevnin is the Manager of Research at the Illinois Law Enforcement Training and Standards Board Executive Institute and Editor of the *Illinois Law Enforcement Executive Forum* at Western Illinois University.

Dr. Sergevnin held several leadership and instructional positions over his career. He is the former Chairperson of the Department of Humanitarian Sciences at the Vladimir Juridical Institute and a Professor at the Saint-Petersburg University. He retired as a Colonel from the Ministry of Internal Affairs (federal police) of Russian Federation. He is a former Senior Research Scholar at the Police Training Institute at the University of Illinois Urbana-Champaign and the former Director of the Illinois Police Corps Academy at Western Illinois University. He has been a visiting professor at Illinois State University and the department of Law Enforcement and Justice Administration at Western Illinois University.

Dr. Sergevnin has published over 60 peer-reviewed journal articles and authored or co-authored nine books pertaining to law enforcement training, leadership, recruitment, history and education.